The RAID® Manual

2001 edition

**A relentlessly positive approach to working with
extreme behaviour, to minimise it at source**

William Davies PhD

First published by The Association for Psychological Therapies 1993
Second edition published by The Association for Psychological Therapies 1998
This edition published by The APT Press in October 2000

British Library Cataloguing-in-Publication Data
A catalogue record to this book is available from the British Library

ISBN: 09520914 6 1

Copyright 1993-2000 by William Davies

Published by The APT Press, P.O.Box 3, Thurnby, Leicester, LE7 9QN, England.

Printed in England by Flexpress, Leicester

Contents

Section Three: RAIDing at the moment of extreme behaviour

Section Four: In conclusion

Section One: Total RAIDing

The challenge we are presented with in Section One is this:

'Please design a service to resolve extreme behaviour; you will not know the nature of the extreme behaviour until after you have designed the service'.

Chapter 1:

What is extreme behaviour?

There is no right or wrong answer to this question. Once, the term 'Challenging Behaviour' was used to refer to any client-behaviour that challenged the organisation which was responsible for coping with it. More recently it is taken to mean just whatever client-behaviour staff or carers find challenging - or difficult - to deal with. Equally it can be taken to mean whatever *the client* finds challenging to deal with. So it can vary a great deal from one person to another.

When I am running the RAID course one of the first things I ask the attenders is what behaviours they find challenging or extreme. I have run the course – and this manual is intended for – people working in prisons, special hospitals, secure units, in residential facilities for people with learning disabilities, for children's home staff, for foster carers, for people working with adults and with youngsters, with foster carers, and with others too. The consistent fact that always amazes me is just what a range of 'extreme behaviours' exist. (And curiously, how little they vary from one setting to another.) For example, any of the following can be included on a list of 'extreme behaviour':

- *Aggression and violence*
- *Destroying property*
- *Self-harm and suicide attempts*
- *Verbal Abuse*
- *Threats*
- *Shouting*
- *Lying*
- *Going to the toilet in public*
- *Lacking sexual inhibitions*
- *Stealing*
- *"Grassing"*
- *Abusing drugs*
- *Frequently seeking medical attention*
- *Spitting*
- *Smearing excrement or putting it in pockets*
- *Bullying*
- *Attacking staff 'weak spots'*
- *Playing staff off against each other / Manipulation*
- *Absconding*
- *Making false allegations*
- *Being negative and apathetic*

And there are others as well! The striking thing is that this is such a long list, and there are so many diverse extreme behaviours. This means that we cannot realistically aim to have a separate strategy for each extreme behaviour. We need <u>an overall philosophy</u> that will lend itself to any of the items on the list.

There are two common philosophies that I have come across, namely (a) punishment and (b) extinction. Before we go on and look at the RAID philosophy I think it's probably worth spending a couple of minutes looking briefly at these two.

The punishment philosophy is probably the most common one that I encounter, even though it's never, or rarely, termed that. The idea is by no means an unreasonable one and in fact is, paradoxically, surprisingly liberal. The idea is that we don't want to dictate to another person what they <u>should</u> do, simply what they <u>should not</u> do. This, in theory, gives them plenty of leeway to behave just as they wish, so long as they avoid certain forbidden behaviours. On the other hand, if they do indulge in the forbidden behaviours, then we produce consequences designed to discourage them from doing so again.

There are of course problems with such an apparently reasonable idea, of which I think the following are the principal ones:

1. <u>What happens when punishment doesn't work</u>? The normal practice is that it is stepped up to a greater level, a bigger punishment. And what happens if that doesn't work? Again it is stepped up even further. This can lead to some very extreme behaviours on the part of the professional. For example, I have seen on a number of occasions a compulsorily-detained patient in a room which contains only a foam-rubber mattress. Nothing else, no furniture, no bed-linen, no clothes even. Just the patient and the mattress. And has this finally got a grip on the problem behaviour? Typically not, the patient is still smearing faeces and indulging in other antisocial behaviours. So the first problem is primarily an ethical one, namely that we as professionals can be led on to more and more extreme responses, all to no effect.

2. The second problem with punishment is purely practical, namely that <u>it frequently produces 'reactance' or 'counter-control'</u> (two terms used to refer to the same thing). The concept is simple enough and observed frequently enough. Namely, the person we are working with reacts against our attempts to control his or her behaviour. Jimmy Boyle in *A Sense of Freedom* describes this phenomenon vividly. He describes how his extreme behaviour in prison met with a range of sanctions - both formal and informal - from the prison authorities and prison staff. This further exacerbated his own behaviour with a result that one person lost his life, another lost his eye, and so on. Effectively, neither side was prepared to 'back down'. The logical result of that is that measure and counter-measure become more and more extreme.

3. If we adopt punishment as our philosophy then we are always 'on the back foot' in the sense that <u>we are always reacting to what the other person does</u>; they set the agenda. We are always being 'reactive' rather than 'proactive'. The problem with this is that it is very wearing for us staff. Most people like to have a good element of 'proactive-ness' in what they do, rather than always having their actions dictated by the person they are working with.

4. But the problem with punishment that strikes me most forcibly is that it is an approach that <u>actually relies upon the person we're working with behaving badly</u> – unless they do, we have no strategy. To me the idea of having an approach for removing extreme behaviour which relies upon the person behaving in an extreme manner is a paradox that I can't bring myself to accept.

So, although punishment and sanctions may be necessary in certain circumstances (and we look at that later on), punishment is an absolute non-starter as an overall 'philosophy of care'. Incidentally, just in case you are thinking that nobody uses punishment as 'a philosophy of care' I'd have to say that I disagree. In my experience, although very few people say or write that their service uses punishment as their prime method, it is nevertheless the case that it is the most common philosophy I come across. The basic question that I am asked is 'What should we do when Alan hits Ben?' Or 'What should our response be when Chris absconds?' Or 'What should we do when Debbie throws her meal on the floor?' All of which are fundamentally punishment-orientated questions. In other words, they wait for the extreme behaviour to occur and ask how it can be stopped from recurring.

The second often-used approach is that of extinction. Again, the idea here is simple enough and, in many ways, very appealing. The concept is to work out what the person gains from the particular extreme behaviour and ensure that he or she ceases to gain that pay-off. The idea is that once the pay-off has been removed then the behaviour will gradually diminish and cease. And this is not just 'an idea', extinction has been demonstrated very convincingly in numerous studies, although largely (by no means entirely) with animals.

The problems with extinction to some extent mirror those with punishment. Namely:

1. It does not allow the staff to be proactive in any real way.
2. It actually hinges on the extreme behaviour occurring, there is no 'intervention' unless the extreme behaviour does occur.

But there is a much more practical problem, and that is for extinction to work you have to have 100% consistency. And that is just crying for the moon; in a group of staff you never get 100% consistency. Come to that, even in an individual you never get 100% consistency. And without that consistency what you have is not 'extinction' but 'intermittent reinforcement' which, unfortunately is the strongest form of reinforcement there is.

<u>Take an example</u>. Supposing you were to work in a residential unit which contains Ed whose extreme behaviour is that he pesters staff. Sometimes he'll pester for something (for example a cup of tea) other times he will keep repeating a particular question (for example, 'Where were you born?') An extinction programme would involve (a) ensuring that Ed never gets a cup of tea when he pesters for it (but does when he asks in a normal way), and (b) ensuring that Ed never gets your attention when he pesters you about where you were born.

Immediately some practical problems arise. For example, what is the difference between 'pestering for a cup of tea' and 'asking for a cup of tea, twice maybe'. Similarly, when Ed asks a newcomer where he was born how do we know - at that first asking - that Ed is going to *repeatedly* ask the newcomer the same question? Such little details make non-response extremely difficult and you're almost bound to get the occasional responses, namely intermittent reinforcement of his pestering.

Additionally, in any group of staff, you are almost bound to find one or more people who - quite reasonably perhaps - say 'well why shouldn't Ed have a cup of tea when he wants one?' which is a further difficulty.

And if you add all that to the fact that if Ed picks up you are trying to manipulate his behaviour in this way there is a good chance he too will exhibit 'counter-control' or 'reactance' in just the same way as if he were receiving punishment. In other words he will pester more, or exhibit some other more extreme behaviour as though he is saying to us 'alright then, try not responding to that!' Furthermore, the example we took was of 'pestering' which is not really a very extreme behaviour. Supposing we had taken the example of 'bullying', it then becomes much more difficult to not respond. So, for all those reasons, extinction is - unfortunately, because it has such good theoretical underpinnings - a non-starter as a philosophy for working with extreme behaviour.

Which all leads us on to the RAID philosophy ...

Chapter 2:

We Need A Clear Philosophy:
The RAID® approach

The RAID® Approach to Difficult or Extreme Behaviour is an eclectic one. The fact that it lays particular emphasis on the Relationship between helper and helped, 'Building' or developing the client, and the Example set by the helper entitles it to be considered a humanistic approach. Equally those with a behavioural background will recognise many of the concepts and phraseology.

The acronym summarises - and exaggerates - the message:

Reinforce Appropriate, 'Ignore' Difficult & disruptive .

In other words, to reinforce appropriate behaviour and ignore – or at least play down – difficult and disruptive behaviour.

I like to picture it as follows:

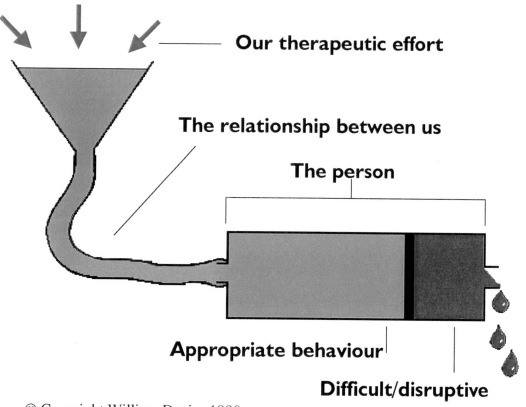

Our therapeutic effort

The relationship between us

The person

Appropriate behaviour

Difficult/disruptive

The person - or client - is represented by the syringe-type tube which is mostly green liquid (Appropriate behaviour) but with some red liquid (Difficult and disruptive behaviour). In a study we conducted at units for people who were impossible to manage in conventional social services and health services facilities - at St Andrews Hospital, Northampton - we found that even the most difficult and disruptive people were behaving perfectly appropriately for 85% or more of the time. Hence the picture above, where the tube contains mostly clear fluid is indeed an accurate reflection.

Our task is to continually top up the green liquid and the allow the red liquid to drip away. Or, to abandon our analogy, to continually work to expand the appropriate behaviour and allow the difficult and disruptive behaviour gradually to diminish and dissipate.

We will examine this more closely through the remaining text, but for the moment several observations are worth making:

1. We do not 'Ignore' the individual, we (usually) simply do not notice - or at least play down - the extreme behaviour

2. Anything to do with safety cannot of course be 'Ignored'

3. It is much more important to reinforce appropriate behaviour than it is to ignore or play down difficult / disruptive.

4. Reinforcing can mean three main things:

- We make a point of being positive focused, we notice predominantly the *good* things that others do, and ask ourselves the question: *'What can I do to make that more likely to happen again?'*

- We try to make 'Green' behaviour reinforcing in itself. For example, if we believe that homework is appropriate behaviour for children, we try to make it enjoyable to do, maybe by keeping the child company, or whatever ingenious means we can think of. (Contrast this with the approach of saying: *'You can watch the TV when you have finished your homework'*, which is tantamount to admitting that homework is akin to a punishment!)

- We try to help the person create a reinforcing life.

WHY RAIDing WORKS

There are many reasons why the RAID® approach works. Research evidence is documented in the RAID® References section, but in some ways it is more important to satisfy ourselves *personally* as to why it works. Only if we are fully convinced will we be able to carry ourselves through the inevitable difficult times that are part and parcel of working with people who display Extreme Behaviours.

EXERCISE

Below, write as many 'common-sense' reasons you can think of for why the RAID® approach might work with your clients:

_____

_____

_____

_____

_____

_____

_____

_____

_____

On the next page there are ten reasons why the approach works. When you read them you will see that each is difficult to argue with, each has 'face-validity'. Nevertheless, to me, the first four are absolutely key ones. The first three form a useful yardstick when we look back over an intervention we have made and ask ourselves whether it was a good one. The fourth provides a yardstick against which to judge the whole ethos of our treatment establishment.

WHY DOES THE RAID® APPROACH WORK?

1.   **It strengthens the relationship between carer and client,** by laying emphasis on appropriate behaviour, rather than involving oneself in non-productive interactions over difficult and disruptive behaviour.

2.   **In the RAID® approach the carer automatically *models* appropriate behaviour.** People tend to copy us rather than necessarily do what we say. Hence, if we habitually criticise an individual this will not so much improve their behaviour as teach that person how to criticise.

3.   **Stressing appropriate behaviour 'builds' the client, makes the client *feel* more competent and less frustrated.** White, in 1959 demonstrated how important feelings of 'self-efficacy' are. Miller et al showed how frustration often results in aggression.

4.   **People will make us take notice of them, so we are best to take notice when they behave appropriately.** As Stewart says *'if you don't give a client positive strokes, they will make you give them negative strokes'.*

5.   **It motivates staff and keeps us thinking in positive terms about clients.** It maintains our motivation by avoiding the frustration of indulging in punitive or unpleasant measures which don't seem to work.

6.   **With the RAID® approach there is simply 'more in it' for the client to behave well rather than badly.** The behavioural DRO (Differential Reinforcement of Other behaviour) paradigm summarises this aspect.

7.   **It allows us to reinforce behaviours *incompatible with* those we are trying to get rid of.** Hence the most effective way of changing the behaviour of a lazy person is not to criticise them when they are sitting down idly, but to reinforce them they are being active.

8.   **It builds on what the client can already do.** And gets the client trying more new behaviours, thanks to the high rate of positive feedback.

9.   **It gives real information.** Whereas criticism only tells us that we have made one error and there are millions of others to make, highlighting 'correct' performance gives hard information on how to do things right, time and time again.

10.   **The RAID® approach minimises the possibility of *countercontrol*.**
This is a phenomenon - 'pushing against us' - well described by Mahoney in his 1974 book, *Cognition and Behaviour Modification*, and one which is especially pertinent in dealing with extreme behaviour.

THE RAID® ACRONYM:

Stands for Reinforce Appropriate, Ignore Difficult or Disruptive. In the previous section we looked at the theory underlying the RAID® approach. There are also clear advantages of having the theory encapsulated in a simple acronym:

- It is easy to remember.

- It enables us to give a clear instruction to ourselves when faced with difficult behaviour.

- It is easy to share with colleagues.

- It enables staff to prompt each other about how to react to green - and difficult - behaviour

Note: The RAID acronym does not tell the whole story. As you will see, there is more to it than simply reinforcing green behaviour and 'ignoring' red. Nevertheless, it does emphasise the theme of our interventions, relentlessly building the person, while playing down other aspects.

Chapter 3:

How To Decide Which Behaviour Is Green

So our philosophy is to spot green behaviour in those we are working with, and to reinforce it. In other words, to spot appropriate behaviour and to nurture it, develop it, expand it. And to play down - or 'ignore' - as much as possible of the red behaviour.

So this suggests that we are going to have to become experts on green behaviour. Knowing what it is and being very skilled at spotting it. Maybe this sounds easy to you, but in my experience it is one of the most difficult things for people to learn. Especially people who have been trained in working with 'challenging behaviour' or 'extreme behaviour' because that's what they think in terms of. They are experts in working with 'challenging behaviour' and can spot it a mile off. So, if that's you, I'm asking you to become equally expert in spotting green behaviour. Actually I'm asking more than that; I'm asking you to become much more expert in spotting green behaviour than you are in spotting extreme behaviour.

What types of green behaviour (appropriate behaviour) are there? Basically there are three types:

1. **'Everyday' green behaviour.**
    This is just exactly what it says. The motto here is: *Anything that is not inappropriate is appropriate.* So, under this heading we might include the following, all depending on just *when* they are being done:

    * Talking to other people
    * Watching television
    * Cooking
    * Playing (football, games etc.)
    * Doing repairs
    * Eating with a knife and fork
    * Using the toilet appropriately
    * Sleeping

    The thing about these - and many more like them - is that they are virtually invisible. Such behaviours are so everyday that we think nothing of them when we see them. On the other hand, when such behaviours disappear, their disappearance becomes very obvious. For instance if we 'reverse' each of the above what we get is the following:

* Isolating himself, refusing to talk to anybody
* Unwilling to indulge in recreational activities such as watching T.V.
* Unable or unwilling to care for herself by cooking
* Does not indulge in pleasurable activities such as play
* Does not maintain or repair his own property
* Uses his hands to eat with
* Urinates in his wardrobe and chest of drawers
* Stays awake at night and is disruptive during the daytime

No doubt you may have read entries very similar to those in case notes of some people that you work with.

So, in summary what we are saying is that <u>it is important that we notice everyday green behaviours and provide a modicum of reinforcement</u> (we will discuss how later on). If we don't then we end up with the problem behaviours in the second bullet list.

2. **Especially-green behaviour**.
Especially-green behaviour is behaviour that actually *contradicts* the extreme behaviour normally exhibited. For example, if Alan normally enjoys winding up Ben, and Ben normally reacts by hitting Alan, especially-green behaviour would be where Alan and Ben are getting on with each other well. Very important to notice, and to respond to in the best way (again, we will discuss how later).

Ironically, this 'especially-green' behaviour can be difficult to spot. This is the more the pity because it is so important that we do spot it. You might have come across the following conundrum in the advertising literature for The RAID Course (and we also come back to it later on in this book): What is wrong with the following sentence? "We notice that whenever Sue harmed herself she had had an argument with her boyfriend just before; in other words, every time they have an argument she harms herself".

The answer is that *the second half of the sentence does not follow from the first.* Whilst it may be true that 'every time Sue harms herself she's had an argument with her boyfriend just before' it is not necessarily true that every time they argue she harms herself. And it is very important that we *do* spot those times that she has had an argument with her boyfriend but has not harmed herself because that is exactly the behaviour we would wish to reinforce. Unfortunately, however, it is difficult to notice. It is much more obvious when Sue does harm herself (and thereby brings it to our attention that she has argued with her boyfriend) than when she doesn't (even though she may have just argued with her boyfriend but we weren't aware of it).

14

I sometimes have people say to me something along the following lines: 'Yes, but I wouldn't reinforce somebody for not harming themselves when they've just had an argument with their boyfriend … that's how it should be anyway'. And a big part of me feels like agreeing with this, that is indeed how it *should* be. On the other hand, for Sue, that is not how it was and, when she argues with her boyfriend without harming herself, she is making substantial progress.

And this perhaps is the key point: especially-green behaviour is characterised by the single word '**progress**'.

3. **'Not quite the shade of green we had in mind, but green nevertheless.'**
   I remember from when I worked in a regional secure unit one particular ward round. We were discussing a woman patient who had been with us for a while and was in danger of becoming institutionalised. The nub of the discussion centred around our feeling that we wanted her to develop more 'autonomy' - to decide for herself what she wanted to do. So we all put forward our various ideas as to how we could go about achieving this and, in truth, I don't think any of them were really acted upon.

   Nevertheless, a few weeks later she was again discussed at length in the ward round. This time she was exhibiting a different problem, namely she was showing a great degree of reluctance to go to particular therapy sessions she was scheduled for, she much preferred to watch T.V. or talk to other patients or just read a magazine. So, again, we all discussed at some length exactly how we might go about persuading her that she wanted to go to the therapy sessions. And then one member of nursing staff said 'but isn't this the woman we were talking about a few weeks ago, the one where we were saying we wanted her to be more autonomous, to decide for herself what she wanted to do?' And we all agreed that this was that self same woman. 'So', he said 'isn't she doing just what we wanted her to do, to decide that she'd prefer to watch T.V. or whatever rather than go to the therapy session?'

   Now this met with a good degree of silence. Of course he was right, the patient was indeed showing the very autonomy we had wanted her to. But we wanted to have our cake and eat it, we wanted her to decide to do the things we wanted her to do! Nevertheless the nurse was quite right and her developing autonomy was probably more important than her attending the particular therapy session. So, although it wasn't quite the shade of green we had in mind, it was nevertheless green and therefore to be reinforced.

   In a similar way, I was talking to a foster carer who had just about lost all her patience with the 11 year old girl she was looking after. She said that, over a period of 2 or 3 days, she had nagged the girl to tidy her room. And still the room was pretty much of a health-hazard. Then, on the third evening, the girl was upstairs and things were quite quiet and the foster carer hoped, and assumed, that she was at last doing as requested. So she went upstairs with every intention of praising her efforts and even joining in doing some tidying. But what she found was the girl sitting in the bath washing her hair.

This led to a prolonged outburst on behalf of the foster carer and this was the main focus of our weekly discussion that week. For ten minutes she'd ranted and raved at the girl, she had in her own words 'completely lost it'.

For want of anything better to say, I asked her why the girl was washing her hair. 'Oh', was the reply 'She was in some school play or other the next morning'.

There again (although it took some time for me to broach this point with the foster carer) what the girl was doing was indeed appropriate. She was making herself look presentable in preparation for the school play she was in. This surely was green behaviour even if not quite the shade of green that the foster carer had in mind. Nevertheless, if it's green it gets reinforced, or should do if we are wise.

So, in summary, it is very important that we are familiar with the kinds of green behaviour that can be exhibited and that we are good at spotting them. For, the very most basic steps in reinforcing green behaviour is first of all to notice it.

Exercise:

Think of someone you work with – a patient or client – and answer the following questions:

What 'everyday green' behaviour does she or he show?

_____

_____

_____

_____

_____

What 'especially-green' behaviour does she or he show?

_____

_____

_____

_____

_____

What 'not quite the shade of green we had in mind, but green nevertheless' behaviour does she or he show?

_____

_____

_____

_____

_____

Exercise rationale:
To increase awareness of green behaviour, for later use.

Chapter 4:

Getting Good At Reinforcing Green Behaviour

What is a reinforcer?

In 1911 Thorndike, in his book *Animal Intelligence*, wrote what came to be known as Thorndike's Law of Effect: *'Behaviours closely followed by rewarding consequences are strengthened and more likely to recur in the future under similar circumstances.'*

This for a while seemed like 'common sense' and proved a useful law of behaviour. However, it did not explain events such as one I came across recently:

Two staff from a children's home told me about a young girl of about 5 or 6 years old who had a severe problem in that she pestered staff much more often than other children, and was thereby disrupting the home quite substantially. One day they saw her happily playing with her toys, and stood watching her for a while. Then, adopting a method similar to the RAID approach, they reasoned that instead of watching her, they should 'go and reward her.' So they went to her, and began to talk and ask her what was happening. No sooner had they done this than she immediately started pestering them.

Their lesson from this was, unfortunately, incorrect. It was, for one of them, 'let sleeping dogs lie', and for the other 'reward doesn't work.'

B.F.Skinner's *'The Behaviour of Organisms'* went some way to answering this by introducing the term reinforcer instead of reward. A reinforcer was defined operationally as <u>a consequence which increases the likelihood of a behaviour occurring again under similar circumstances</u>.

Using this as a criterion, the two staff in question had not reinforced the young girl's behaviour, they had disrupted it. In that case, what was reinforcing her play? There are two answers:

- Her play was *intrinsically* reinforcing. She just enjoyed playing with the toys, no other reinforcer was necessary.
- The staff were reinforcing simply by watching. This will come as no surprise to anyone who has worked with children or brought up their own ... there is nothing youngsters like more than that you 'come and watch'!

It also explains a finding with a woman with learning difficulties and aggressive outbursts whose care I was once involved with. The ward staff were adopting our usual approach: in other words they were praising her for appropriate behaviour, and tending to play down her aggressive episodes. It was not working; rather her aggression seemed to be getting more frequent and severe, if anything. Not expecting a great deal of light to be shed, I had a talk with her. Mainly we talked of things in general ... her life outside, how she liked things inside the hospital, and so on. In discussing the latter, her most vehement statement was 'I wish they wouldn't keep saying 'well done' 'They' referring to us staff.

What to us was 'social reinforcement' was to her manipulation and condescension, though she did not use those words. It was as though, each time a member of staff said *'Well done'*, she made a mental note not to repeat whatever it was that had produced such praise.

In other words, reinforcers are only reinforcing if they reinforce. It is not how we - the staff - see it, it is how the recipient perceives it that counts. So, reinforcers work, we just need to find the right ones: the staff working with the young girl were able to settle simply to watching her play, on occasions, and we were able to find a gentler form of social reinforcement for the woman with aggressive outbursts.

What types of reinforcers are there?

There are two broad categories of reinforcer:
Positive ... and ... **Negative.**

Positive reinforcement almost always means giving someone something they like in order to make them more likely to do a particular behaviour again. For example, if we see a resident 'keep their cool' in spite of another resident deliberately winding them up during a mealtime, we might give a faint smile, or an acknowledging ('well done') look, or whatever. We might expect this would encourage them to keep their cool next time something like that happens.

Negative reinforcement is probably the most mis-defined term in psychology. In fact it is straightforward enough, the only thing we have to remember is that it too reinforces behaviour ... makes it more likely to happen again. How? <u>By taking away something the client does not like</u>. So, in the example above, we might reinforce the client keeping his cool by telling him he need not do the washing up after the meal, even though it is his turn.

Importantly, in spite of the terminology, there is nothing 'superior' about positive reinforcement when compared with negative reinforcement. Indeed, many people are much more responsive to negative reinforcement, even though most people rarely think of using it deliberately. (Equally, many people respond best to positive reinforcement.)

Types of Positive Reinforcer

There are several recognised categories of possible positive reinforcers, namely:

Social
Social reinforcers are 'natural', immediate, and, usually, non-disruptive to the behaviour we are trying to encourage. They include: touch, taps, cuddles, affection, praise, chat, attention, trips out, smiles, eye-contact, nods, winks, particular facial expressions. And many more.

Food and other Consumables
Food, Drinks, Sweets, cigarettes.

High-Probability Behaviours
These are behaviours that the individual naturally spends a lot of time doing. Examples might include: smoking, watching Coronation Street on TV, spending time with a particular staff member, cooking, sitting quietly alone.

Points/Plastic/Tokens
Tokens or points that can exchanged for something at a later date, eg at the end of the week These can (a) make more immediate a later reinforcer, and (b) add more substance to social reinforcement. They can also be formalised into 'programmes'. See Formal RAIDing for details.

Feedback
Feedback is a powerful, if insufficiently used, reinforcer. Few interventions rely solely on feedback; normally, positive feedback would be associated with some other reward in addition. Some arcade games however, notably driving-type ones, rely on feedback as the only reinforcer.

Note: Feedback, potentially a very powerful influence indeed, highlights the importance of the relationship between carer and client. How will the client react to feedback from us if they don't like us? At best with indifference, at worst counter to the way we want. Likewise, how will a client react to feedback if they suspect we do not like them? Can they really trust such feedback?

Negative Reinforcement

Negative reinforcement is to reinforce behaviour by letting the client out of doing something. (Although many people who enter the lottery do so to win money they will spend on positive reinforcers - big house, fast car, lavish holidays - some do so in the hope of negative reinforcement - being able to give up work, or money-worries disappearing.)

So, we might reinforce a client by allowing them to skip doing the washing up if it were their turn, or to skip doing other chores, or to miss a particular therapy session they don't like, or whatever.

Accidental negative reinforcement

One important problem sometimes arises when we try to move a client from a high-dependency unit to a lower-dependency one where they have less supervision and perhaps have to make their own meals. Some clients effectively block this move by behaving in a disruptive fashion - smashing things up, attacking others, so that they have to be kept in the high-dependency unit. In fact their disruptive behaviour is negatively reinforced - as a result of it they avoid having to go to the new, low-dependency unit. There is of course only one solution to this: we have to - somehow or other - get the client to *want* to move to the new unit.

The Timing of Reinforcement

Giving attention and reward is a great start, but we do better still if we take a second to ask 'Just exactly what is happening?' before rewarding. We try our best not to reward behaviour which is against the client's interests.

One unit established a reinforcement system for a resident who had trouble sleeping. If he had a good night - defined as sleeping through the night - the gave him a star to acknowledge that fact. The problem was that they gave him the star when he came downstairs for his breakfast in the morning. Clearly there is a possible problem here, in that he may (consciously or unconsciously) connect the star and associated praise with coming downstairs rather than sleeping through the night.

If at all possible, we try to make reinforcement immediate.

You sometimes hear it said: *'We've tried everything with him, but nothing seems to reinforce his behaviour.'* Rarely, however, has <u>negative</u> reinforcement – reinforcing the behaviour through letting the person out of doing something he doesn't like – been tried systematically. Very few people are skilled in the use of negative reinforcement.

Beware: Negative reinforcement is probably the most mis-used term in psychology. It has nothing to do with punishment, it is the technique of reinforcing (strengthening) a behaviour by letting the person out of doing something he does not like doing.

Chapter 5:

Learning How To 'Ignore' Red Behaviour.

When somebody produces difficult or disruptive behaviour, the best policy is to ignore it - or at least play it down - unless, for whatever reason, it really cannot be ignored. (See *What We Can't Ignore*, later). By ignoring what we mean is:

1.　　Act as though we did not notice the disruptive behaviour, but on the other hand ……

2.　　Take care that the client does not gain immediate reinforcement.

In summary, if a client produces difficult or disruptive behaviour it is probably best that they do not receive any positive outcome for doing so.

On the other hand we do not 'send them to Coventry' or 'give them the silent treatment', we simply act as though we didn't notice whatever the disruptive behaviour was. Even more than that, we genuinely do not allow that behaviour to annoy us. We 'let it go', 'don't get latched into it', or whatever phrase we like to use. That way, if the client produces some *green* behaviour shortly afterwards, we are ready and willing to gently reinforce that behaviour.

It is perhaps worth clarifying why we do this - why we ignore difficult behaviour. If you are of a behavioural orientation you may say it is extinction, but I do not think this is it. Extinction requires complete non-responding, and my experience of treatment units suggests that this rarely if ever occurs ... there is always someone, either staff or another client, who will respond to the difficult behaviour, at least occasionally.

Rather the purpose is so that we do not get embroiled in disagreements and 'nit-picking' which wears down the relationship between us and encourages the client to indulge in 'reactance', ie to resist our attempts to help. Furthermore, ignoring (or playing down) the red behaviour makes us focus on where the real action is, namely in reinforcing the adaptive stuff.

As in the earlier example, it is much more important to spot the occasions where a client controls himself and resists the temptation to respond to a wind-up than it is to go on at the person when he does explode in response to such wind-ups. Such a course of action truly 'builds' the client, which is what we are trying to do. The alternative suggests to the client that not only are other clients getting at him, staff are too!

Chapter 6:

The more rewarding the person's life is, the less extreme will be their behaviour

 EXERCISE

Below are some dream statements. Rate how true they are for your clients by circling the appropriate response.

BIOLOGICAL FACTORS

- My clients have a generally settled 'biological routine'. By that I mean they go to bed and get up at roughly the same time most nights, and those times are 'reasonable' times - they have not 'turned night into day and day into night'.

Very true   *A little true*   *Not really true*   *False*

- My clients obtain sufficient sleep, and this occurs at night, not in the day

Very true   *A little true*   *Not really true*   *False*

- My clients have a generally settled biological routine in terms of eating too. By that I mean they have their meals at roughly the same time every day.

Very true   *A little true*   *Not really true*   *False*

- My clients receive about the right amount of nutrition. By that I mean they not only eat regularly, but the diet is reasonably *nutritious*. Their calories come from reasonable food, and not from, say, alcohol. They neither under-eat or over-eat.

Very true   *A little true*   *Not really true*   *False*

- My clients do not abuse drugs. By this I refer not only to 'street' or 'recreational' drugs, but also 'endemic' drugs such as alcohol, caffeine (in coffee, tea, and Cola drinks), and nicotine. Whilst they may consume some or all of these, it it done in moderation (20 units of alcohol per week, 3 to 4 cups of coffee/tea/Cola in total per day, 15 cigarettes per day).[1]

Very true   *A little true*   *Not really true*   *False*

- My clients get plenty of exercise every day

Very true   *A little true*   *Not really true*   *False*

- My clients know how to relax, and are able to do so when they wish.

Very true   *A little true*   *Not really true*   *False*

BEHAVIOURAL FACTORS

- My clients have sufficient enjoyable[2] activities to do, and these activities are not over-demanding or unduly anxiety-provoking

Very true   *A little true*   *Not really true*   *False*

- Activities are known well in advance so that there is no undue apprehension about 'what is in store'.

Very true   *A little true*   *Not really true*   *False*

- My clients are generally able to schedule their time (or it is planned this way for them) so that relatively less enjoyable tasks ('chores') are generally soon followed by more enjoyable ones.

Very true   *A little true*   *Not really true*   *False*

---

[1] We of course recognise that smoking is extremely hazardous. Equally we recognise the difficulty that addicts experience in giving up.

[2] In a survey by Michael Argyle, the two most enjoyable activities for adults in the UK were reading and gardening. Reading may not of course refer to books, but may be magazines, newspapers, comics, etc.

- Sometimes my clients have 'treats' randomly, even if they don't 'deserve' them!

Very true   *A little true*   *Not really true*   *False*

- My clients feel part of a team. Not just that they are being 'looked after' they get to feel they have a useful role. This leads to a feeling of empowerment on their part.

Very true   *A little true*   *Not really true*   *False*

ENVIRONMENTAL FACTORS

- My clients get to live in an environment which looks nice and sounds good. There is plenty of variety in colour, and no raucous sudden noisy sounds.

Very true   *A little true*   *Not really true*   *False*

- My clients get to listen to music which makes them feel good: sometimes relaxing, sometimes cheerful and energy promoting.

Very true   *A little true*   *Not really true*   *False*

- My clients watch films and television programmes which have a good effect on them. They tend to avoid ones which model aggression and less desirable human characteristics, also avoiding 'exaggerated self-efficacy' ('only one man could save the ship/bus/world') films.

Very true   *A little true*   *Not really true*   *False*

- I have given real thought to how to satisfy my clients' need to touch and be touched, and this is fulfilled as far as possible.

Very true   *A little true*   *Not really true*   *False*

- My clients eat food which is enticing, has plenty of variety, and makes them feel cared for.

Very true   *A little true*   *Not really true*   *False*

- Although my clients may never go skiing or ride motor cycles, they sometimes have activities which provide the same feeling of exhilaration and bodily vitality.

Very true   *A little true*   *Not really true*   *False*

SOCIAL FACTORS

- I try to ensure that each of my clients has a genuinely close relationship with at least one other person; a relationship where they can confide in each other and talk about their secret hopes or aspirations.

Very true   *A little true*   *Not really true*   *False*

- Where appropriate I support my clients in their developing a physically close relationship with one other person.

Very true   *A little true*   *Not really true*   *False*

- I try to ensure that my clients are not 'socially isolated', in that they have enough people to talk to and to mix socially with.

Very true   *A little true*   *Not really true*   *False*

- Where a client is missing someone, or there has been a big change in their social situation, I ensure that he or she is gently supported through that period, even if it is a long period of time.

Very true   *A little true*   *Not really true*   *False*

EXERCISE

Part One:

By reference to the previous exercise, show how the service you provide for your clients fulfils many of the criteria for 'providing a rewarding a life'.

_____

_____

_____

_____

_____

_____

_____

Part Two:

By reference to the previous exercise, show how you could make your clients' lives even more rewarding. Be very specific, avoid generalities, say exactly what you should do.

_____

_____

_____

_____

_____

_____

_____

Chapter 7:

Rules, Ground-rules and Expectations; necessary, but which are best?

(IF PEOPLE DON'T KNOW WHAT'S EXPECTED OF THEM, THEY PROBABLY WON'T DO IT!)

Thomas Hobbes in his Leviathan (1651) said that the life of man in a natural state, without laws or government, would be 'solitary, poor, nasty, brutish and short.' Both before and since, many people have expended great effort deciding what makes the difference between good and bad rules and laws. It is sad that, in the 1990s, the whole concept of rules is glibly tossed aside as 'institutionalisation' by some.

I suggest that it is a case for Aristotle's 'golden mean'. Surely too many rules and constraints can stifle the development of the person, but equally too few leads to chaos. There is a peak somewhere in between which leads to order, a clear picture of what is right, along with empowerment of the person and a development of his or her autonomy.

But is 'rules' the best word? It is not a bad word, but the problem with it is that it leads us naturally to talk in terms of the red ... those things it would be better for the person not to do ... and then slap a 'not' in front. We also go on to think in terms of sanctions when the 'rule' is broken.

Use the word 'expectations' on the other hand and we immediately talk of the green behaviour ... what is 'Appropriate' in our RAID acronym. We thereby paint a picture of the very thing the person is best to do, rather than a picture of what they are best not doing. And such pictures are all-important.

In summary, it is important to have rules / guidelines / ground-rules / expectations or whatever, and expectations is probably the best word to use because:

- **Expectations point us (and clients) in the direction of *Green* behaviour, whereas rules point us towards the inappropriate.**

- **If people fail to achieve the expectations we set, we *encourage* them to do so. If people break our rules, we think in terms of sanctions.**

- **If we specify our expectations, we paint a picture of 'Appropriate' behaviour. When we specify rules, we usually paint a picture of maladaptive behaviour and simply slap a 'not' or 'don't' in front.** *The mind has no picture of 'not's and 'don'ts'*

And it is right that we do have clear expectations of clients, make it clear how people are meant to behave in our service, or whatever setting we work in. Expectations enable everyone to know where they stand, pre-empt allegations of unfairness (one of the most common *cries de coeur* from clients) and generally define the 'A' of the RAID acronym. They tell us all what is Appropriate.

An absence of a clear specification of how people are meant to behave, on the other hand, although sometimes justified on the grounds of 'de-institutionalisation' is far from what it produces. Staff still have expectations of how clients should behave, but what develops is a myriad of conflicting, unwritten, expectations: some staff believing one thing, other staff believing another. As a result they can be wide open to 'manipulation' from clients of the 'Richard lets me' type. Conversely, it is difficult for clients to know where they stand in the absence of clearly specified expectations.

What we really want are *good* expectations. This means ones that are:

- *agreed upon by all staff*
- *achievable by clients and fair to them*
- *phrased positively whenever we can, saying what clients should do, rather than what they should not do*
- *in clear language, or possibly in picture form*
- *written down, with a copy given to and explained to every client, whenever possible*[3]

If we follow these aims, especially the one about expectations being phrased positively, clients can start towards achieving them. Negatively-written expectations, on the other hand, can never really be achieved.

---

[3] Some clients are not verbal, they can neither read, speak, nor easily understand the spoken word. In such cases 'signing' can sometimes be useful, as can cartoons and photographs. I particularly like the last two. For example, the dining room might have one or two giant, blown-up photographs of all the clients sitting properly at their places eating their own food, and looking happy. Whilst this does not of course guarantee that such a blissful situation will be replicated daily, it does gently 'describe' what is ideal.

An example of how expectations might be written down follows on the next page.

It is for an imaginary residential facility. Some of the timings are vague, for example breakfast is between 8 and 9am. Similarly in the morning clients are meant to do 'something useful' and some examples are given..

In some settings it would be perfectly feasible to use such a sheet as a back up to a friendly talk in which you explain to a new resident how the home works. In a non-residential service, expectations would be quite different, naturally. Nevertheless they do need explaining. Likewise if you work with non-verbal clients you may want to convey what is expected by the use of pictures rather than words. This can be excellently done, vividly and entertainingly. See the dining-room example above as one example.

An example of a therapeutic day in a unit for adults with mental health problems and extreme behaviour

7am	GET UP, SHOWER, SHAVE
8am	BREAKFAST
9-10.30am	COMMUNITY MEETING
11-12.30pm	CHOICE OF THERAPY GROUPING: (a) attend the problem-solving group (b) attend the substance awareness group (c) attend the mental health issues group
1pm	LUNCH, RELAX, TALK
2.30-4.30pm	CHOICE OF USEFUL ACTIVITY, eg: (a) cooking (b) current affairs group (c) gardening (d) music
6pm	TEA. RELAX. TALK
7pm	RECREATION e.g. Video, TV, read/mags., talk, football, pool
8pm	}
	}
9pm	}
	}
10pm	}
11pm	TOILET, TEETH, BED

Notes:

1. Treat each other as you would like to be treated yourself ... including staff!

2. If you have problems or are unhappy, be sure to talk to staff.

3. Treat property with respect; ask if you want to borrow anything; try to look after things.

4. Which TV channel we watch is decided by a vote, or by a member of staff if there is a tie.

5. Smoke only in smoking area.

EXERCISE

1. What word(s) does your service use when explaining things to clients: Rules / Expectations / Boundaries / Guidelines / some other ....

2. How well does your service's expectations match up with these guidelines for setting *good* expectations?

- *agreed upon by all staff*

- *achievable by clients and fair to them*

- *phrased positively whenever we can, saying what clients should do, rather than what they should not do*

- *in clear language, or possibly in picture form*

- *written down, with a copy given to and explained to every client, whenever possible*

3. What could you do to help clients have a clearer more vivid idea of what 'green' behaviour is? Ie a clearer idea of what is expected of them. Remember:

IF PEOPLE DON'T KNOW WHAT'S EXPECTED OF THEM, THEY
PROBABLY WON'T DO IT!

_____

_____

_____

_____

_____

_____

_____

_____

Chapter 8:

Keeping Your Criticisms Constructive, And Your Injunctions Positive.

(Talk Green, Not Red)

Don't Tell People What Not to Do(!)

Constructive criticism differs from standard criticism in that, whereas the latter simply describes the problem, the former gives the solution.

So the following might be examples:

Standard criticism: *'the trouble with you is you don't take enough trouble over things.'*

Constructive criticism: ***'you would do a lot better if you took just a bit more care over that.'***

Standard criticism: *'you are too aggressive to your colleagues.'*

Constructive criticism: ***'your colleagues would like you better if you were a bit more tolerant.'***

Standard criticism: *'your personal hygiene is really bad.'*

Constructive criticism: ***'you would do well to make sure you have a shower every day.'***

The reason why constructive criticism is so much more powerful than standard criticism is that it actively prompts the required behaviour, it points the recipient in the direction of a solution, rather than simply complaining.

Exercise on Constructive Criticism

For each of the following examples of standard criticism, try to write
an matching sentence of constructive criticism.

Standard criticism: *'The trouble with you is you are much too quiet and shy.'*

Constructive criticism:

Standard criticism: *'Your trouble is you worry too much.'*

Constructive criticism:

Standard criticism: *'What you do wrong is you stay up too late, so you are always
                          tired.'*

Constructive criticism:

Standard criticism: *'I wish you wouldn't always contradict me in public.'*

Constructive criticism:

Positive Injunctions

Positive injunctions are akin to constructive criticism. They are simply instructions phrased positively rather than negatively. Again, like constructive criticism, positive injunctions automatically sew the seed of improved behaviour.

Examples:

Negative injunction: *'don't always shout when you're complaining.'*

Positive injunction: **'try to keep your voice a bit more controlled when you are complaining.'**

Negative injunction: *'don't wolf your food.'*

Positive injunction: **'try to eat at the same speed as everybody else.'**

Negative injunction: *'stop grumbling at Gary.'*

Positive injunction: **'try to be friendly to Gary'**

So again, positive injunctions - like constructive criticism - suggest positive behaviour which is then open to natural reinforcement.

Exercise on Positive Injunctions: For each of the following negative injunctions, try to write an matching positive one:

Negative injunction: *'Don't rip your clothes.'*

Positive injunction:

Negative injunction: *'You two - don't play on the road!'*

Positive injunction:

Negative injunction: *'Don't bite your nails.'*

Positive injunction:

Negative injunction: *'Don't be in so much of a hurry.'*

Positive injunction:

Chapter 9:

The Rubber Tube… A Really Good Relationship

WITHOUT A GOOD RELATIONSHIP WE WON'T CONNECT WITH THE CLIENT

There are two ways in which we can improve our relationship with clients: by our own personal efforts, or by altering the system our service operates.

EXERCISE: OUR OWN PERSONAL EFFORTS

Below is a list of the qualities that are useful in developing helping relationships. Go through the whole list rating yourself on each one by placing a number from 1 (bad) to 10 (good) alongside each. This is an exercise you might like to come back from time to time.

- I am energetic and optimistic.

- I am persistent ... I do not give up easily.

- I have the ability to form a collaborative alliance with the client.

- I am gentle, I do not lecture or harangue

- I have the ability to listen.

- I have a professional manner

- I show ingenuity, thinking of good ideas for tackling problems.

- I have a lightness of touch, I'm not too solemn.

- I have the ability to help the client to develop a commitment to change.

- I am genuine.

- I have the ability to make things happen.

- I accept clients and value them.

- I understand each client's problems and 'where they're coming from'.

- I show an appropriate degree of warmth, is neither remote nor 'over-does it'.

But our own personal efforts are not the whole story. Many services operate a 'key-worker' system. It is often the details of this system which determine how successful it is. For example, how is the key-worker allocated to the client? Below are two alternative options:

OPTION ONE

'Our system is that, when we admit a new client, we look to see which member of staff does not have a key client. That member of staff takes on that new client, forms a good relationship with him or her and works to help them improve. This system works because we trust our staff to be professional enough to develop relationships without fear or favour. In other words it does not matter whether they have a natural liking for each other, the staff member will work to take account of that.'

OPTION TWO

'Our system is that, when we have a new client, we allocate a provisional key worker. We then watch to see who the client naturally forms good relationships with and allocate two of those members of staff to work with him or her. This is a professional system and works because it takes account of natural 'chemistry'. It is also good to have two key workers because it prevents one staff member feeling overly responsible for the client, and gives both someone to discuss things with.'

 EXERCISE

Please answer the following questions:

- *Which of the two systems above do you think is likely to be more effective?*

- *Which of the two systems above most closely resembles practice in your service?*

- *Could there be a better system still for your service? If so what is it?*

- *How can you introduce the best system possible for your own service?*

Chapter 10:

Rubber Tube II: Your Personal Qualities

IT'S OUR 'PERSONALITY' THAT REALLY MAKES THINGS HAPPEN

So now we have a clear philosophy of care, which we will expand through this book. But anyone who has been in a helping role will know that philosophy and technique is only half the story, if that. Some people seem to be effective even with the most scanty of plans, while others seem able to pluck defeat from the jaws of victory no matter what.

Crits-Christoph et al looked at the effect of psychological treatments in four big centres in the United States, examined the variance in results and found that the therapist accounted for eight times more variance than the treatment technique used. To simplify only a little, it is eight times more important who treats an individual than what technique is employed.

A graphic example of how therapists can effect their clients was published by Ricks in 1974 who looked at what had become of a group of adolescent boys who had been treated some years previously when they were experiencing very high degrees of anxiety, vulnerability, feelings of unreality and isolation. The boys had been seen by one of two therapists in a child guidance clinic. The long term outcome produced by these two therapists was no different for less disturbed boys, but there was a very large difference in the outcomes with the more disturbed boys.

One therapist, whom Ricks labelled 'supershrink' produced an outcome whereby only 27% of his cases became schizophrenic in adulthood. Those cases seen by therapist B, later labelled 'pseudoshrink', however, yielded an 84% rate of schizophrenia in adulthood. (Bear in mind, when thinking of these as very high rates, that Ricks was only looking at what happened to the more disturbed individuals.) Although the clients were not randomly assigned between therapists A and B, the caseloads were similar.

Ricks looked at the differences in styles between therapist A and therapist B. It transpired that therapist A devoted far more time to those who were disturbed, while the less successful therapist, B, did the opposite. Therapist A, supershrink, tended to be firm and direct with parents, supported the youngsters' increasing independence, and helped them develop problem-solving capabilities for everyday life. All against the background of a strong therapeutic relationship.

Therapists B, pseudoshrink, on the other hand moved rapidly into 'deep material' and Ricks speculates that he may have increased the youngsters' feelings of anxiety, vulnerability, unreality and alienation, without being able to help the boys develop ways of coping with those feelings.

Similarly Luborsky et al (1985) describe their analysis of the outcome of clients seen by nine different therapists. Importantly, treatment manuals were used to guide the delivery of the comparison treatments. In other words, not only were therapists trained to deliver the prescribed treatment, but their work was supervised and monitored to check they were doing what was intended. One might reasonably assume that individual differences between therapists were therefore minimised. Even so, in spite of this careful selection, training, monitoring and supervision, therapists displayed highly divergent results. The patients of therapist A, for example (a different individual from supershrink) showed substantial improvement on a wide variety of outcomes, while C's patients averaged little improvement and on some criteria actually showed an average negative change.

In summary, we not only need a good philosophy of care - for example the RAID approach - but we also need to keep up to scratch on our personal characteristics!.

The research is a bit weak on just what are the best characteristics to have, and in any case it may vary from job to job. You might like to think what characteristics would best suit a person to your job, before going on to the next page to see my own favourites.

SOME SUGGESTIONS AS TO **EXEMPLARY PERSONAL QUALITIES** IN HELPERS:

The following list is partly based on research, partly on my own personal experiences, so you might like to take it as such:

- **Liking people** seems to be important. Sometimes this is referred to as 'valuing', sometimes as 'unconditional positive regard', but maybe both of those words and phrases cloud the issue somewhat. Perhaps it is simply more important to like who we work with. For example, if we work with children, it is important that we tend to like children!

- **Empathy**, or the ability to imagine and understand the other person's position and feelings, probably has a claim to be the paramount characteristic.

- **The ability to make others feel good** is central to reinforcing, and therefore has to be in our list.

- **Being positive, optimistic, and enthusiastic,** are all qualities which can rub off on others and generally build the morale of a group.

- **Determination and persistence** mesh well with the above, to ensure we maintain our enthusiasm, and do not simply have it in bursts!

- **Being able to make things happen.** You know how some people tell a person what to do and they do it? Not because there is the slightest threat, just the way it is said. That.

- **Reliability** goes down well with both clients and colleagues. It covers a multitude of virtues, from simply being there, not too often late or ill, to doing what we say.

- **Team spirit** likewise seems to be a universal winner, both in terms of *offering* help to others and in making them feel effective by *seeking* it.

Of course this list is as inexhaustive as it is idiosyncratic, but the point remains that it is these kind of personal qualities - along with a good philosophy of care - which really make things happen.

Chapter 11:

RAIDing GROUPS

Imagine this situation: you are sitting at a meal with several clients, two of whom are arguing with each other. Loudly, and vehemently. Then one of them 'comes to their senses', apparently sees how disruptive and noisy s/he is being, makes a conscious decision to stop arguing, and, quietly gets on with the meal in spite of continued rather vicious sniping from the other.

What do you, as the responsible member of staff, say? Perhaps more to the point, who do you speak to?

The very question gives the game away, perhaps, but the point is that many - probably the overwhelming majority - of staff would 'have a go' at the one who continued arguing. It seems the obvious thing to do; it is s/he who is drawing attention to themselves. The one who is now quiet has suddenly become invisible!

The more effective strategy is to reinforce the green behaviour of the person who stopped arguing. How? Maybe just by a look or half a smile; maybe something more obvious is needed. Whatever, it needs to be in a way which does not wind up the person who is still arguing. In essence it is just an extension of the RAID approach: Ignoring (or 'letting go') of the arguing, but Reinforcing the Appropriate behaviour of the one who stopped.

A Couple of Points:
Always remember, the purpose of reinforcing the one who is behaving appropriately is not to 'get at' the disruptive one. It really is to reinforce the green behaviour being displayed. If we do that, the other one really will learn from it; and it won't take him too long. Hopefully, it won't always be the same person who gets the plaudits - the reinforcement. If it is, s/he soon becomes thought of as our favourite. And that will work against everyone.

This Approach Can Be Extended Very Effectively:
In talking generally to our clients we can talk about the behaviour of other people - in either positive or negative terms. So we might, for example, say to Tim: 'John's doing well isn't he ... he has really got a grip on himself these days, he used always to be getting into fights and hitting other residents but now he is controlling himself well, he hasn't hit anyone for weeks and weeks.' Or 'That was bad that Sam didn't let Jo have that paper, wasn't it ... Sam wasn't using it, so could have easily let Jo have it.'

This is a powerful way of spelling out approval and disapproval for different behaviours - teaching people the difference between right and wrong - and can be a very effective influence on most people.

However there are a couple of traps ...

Trap 1:

We may seem to be 'gossiping' or 'playing off' one person against another.
One way round this is to confine our positive and negative remarks to characters in TV programmes, or books/magazines/comics, or 'someone I once knew'. In this respect, characters in programmes such as Neighbours, Coronation Street, or other 'soaps' can be ideal. We can comment on what they do with impunity, whilst still getting across - naturally and with no hint of manipulation - what is commendable and what is unacceptable.

Trap 2:

We fall into the temptation of using this as a means of 'getting at' a client. For example if we know that the person we're talking to is very reluctant to let other people have things even if s/he is not using them, it is very tempting - but counterproductive - to say, in an apparently innocent voice: 'Wasn't that nasty of Jo not to let Sam have that, even though Jo had finished with it.'

There is no chance that person we're talking to will be fooled by this ploy. He or she will know well that we are simply getting at them and will react accordingly. If we use this approach as something which genuinely helps people see clearly what is right and what is wrong, however, it is a powerful technique.

Section Two: Targeted RAIDing

Chapter 12:

Points, Tokens, And Those Kind Of Things

Chapter 13:

Reinforcing The *Absence* Of Behaviour

Chapter 14:

Asking Green Questions, Answering Them, and Producing a RAID Treatment Plan

Chapter 15:

Getting the Person Looking to the Future (That Means Putting More Green Into The Funnel)

Chapter 16:

What To Do If You Can Work Out What He Or She Is Getting Out Of Behaving Red

Chapter 17:

What To Do If You Can Work Out What Is Triggering The Red Behaviour

Chapter 18:

Working Out What Purpose Is Served By Behaving Red And working Out What Is Triggering The Red Behaviour

Chapter 19:

Some Sort Of A Summary

Chapter 12:

Points, Tokens, And Those Kind Of Things

So far we have talked only of 'informally' being more rewarding when a client behaves positively, and less rewarding at other times. RAIDing in other words.

We can however set up formal RAID systems for three different scenarios:

- To reinforce simple green behaviour, eg. a client attending occupational therapy sessions or other treatment interventions.

- To reinforce green behaviour which is actually incompatible with a difficult or disruptive behaviour, eg. rewarding Alan for being friendly to Ben when normally he is antagonistic to him.

- Reinforcing the absence of a particular difficult behaviour, eg. reinforcing not swearing or not pestering.

The first two of these are relatively straightforward. We settle ourselves down with the client, agree just what behaviour it is we are going to reinforce, and how we are going to reinforce it. The aim is to have a good atmosphere in order to achieve something that will be in the client's interests and within their capabilities.

Very often the reinforcer will be either a token (eg. counters or pieces of card of some sort) or points; which are normally recorded on a piece of paper, or some sort of 'blocks' which are charted on a large sheet, or gold stars or similar. Usually these tokens/points/blocks/stars are exchangeable for something. So, for example, five gold stars might be exchangeable for one Mars Bar.

A slightly more sophisticated system arises where - in the above example - five gold stars are exchangeable for a Mars Bar plus a black star. And, say, five black stars are exchangeable for a trip to the cinema. This way our clients benefit both in the short term - with the Mars Bar - and in the longer term - by accumulating black stars for trips to the cinema.

Some staff have strong feelings against points and tokens, in which case there is no obligation to devise an intervention which relies upon them. However, one of the important side-effects of such a system is that it gets the client thinking of the future. We shall see later that this is very important in several ways, but for the moment we can summarise it in this sentence: *'If there is no tomorrow for a client, he can be as disruptive as he wants today'*.

If you take the example of rewarding the occurrence of a dry bed, in the case of someone who suffers from nocturnal enuresis, we might have a system whereby one dry night is rewarded with a blue star, two of which can be swapped for a Mars Bar. You also might have an added refinement which says that five blue stars *in a row* can be swapped for a black star, and two black stars result in a cinema trip. By doing this we can encourage *reliable* green behaviour.

There was a nice example of natural formal RAIDing in a school for children with emotional and behavioural difficulties. Teachers were able to give out pink certificates for examples of appropriate behaviour; all they had to do was to fill in what the behaviour was. That in itself was rewarding for many children, even though the certificates were not worth anything tangible, they were just an indication that the teacher had recognised the youngster's effort. But an embellishment was built in whereby five pink certificates could be exchanged for a blue certificate, and a blue certificate could be exchanged for something tangible, and there was a list of the possibilities. Furthermore, blue certificates were given out by the Head, in front of the whole school.

In general the key factors we have to watch out for are:

◆ **That the client can achieve the behaviour we aim for.**

◆ **That the reward is one the client wants!**

◆ **That the reward is in proportion to what the client achieves.**

Chapter 13:

Reinforcing The *Absence* Of Behaviour

Things start to get slightly more sophisticated when we begin to reinforce the absence of particular behaviours. For example, when we want to reinforce not swearing or not pestering. Such behaviours - swearing and pestering - normally have us thinking in terms of fines or sanctions of one sort or another. But there is a more effective, positive, RAIDing approach to it which is not difficult to implement.

Take the example of a six year old boy who had developed the habit of swearing, and especially using the word 'f***ing'. So he would say to his mother, for example, 'Make me a f***ing cup of tea'. Not only did this take place in the domestic situation but also in public. The net result was that his mother was not content to simply ignore the behaviour and reward other, good aspects of his behaviour.

The problem, therefore, was to construct a positive intervention, but one that satisfied the mother's need to intervene in some way each time her son swore.

The solution was to 'give' the son a vertical column of eleven blocks per day which were drawn out on a large chart. Each time he swore, one of the eleven blocks was simply crossed through by the mother, starting at the top of the column. It was estimated that - before intervention - the youngster was swearing about twelve times per day so it was deemed to be an achievable goal to cut that down to ten times. It was therefore agreed with the child that so long as there was one block un-crossed-through at the end of the day he could have a bite sized Mars Bar. (This was a potent reinforcer for him!)

This satisfied the mother's need to intervene (cross off a block) when her son swore, but she was also keen for him to have his bite sized Mars Bar. The result was that the mother and child worked in unison to achieve the desired - positive - goal.

Once the child was regularly achieving the ten-a-day target then the number of blocks was cut down to eight with the procedure as before. Once the eight-a-day was achieved it was cut down to six, and so on down to zero.

Clearly, such a procedure can apply, in one form or another to people of varying ages and capabilities.

Note: This example raises an important point, namely that it seems not to be in the boy's interests to eliminate swearing completely ... if he does that, he is 'cured' and his Mars bar programme disappears, and he loves Mars bars! The answer in this instance is simple enough: keep giving him the occasional Mars bar even when his swearing has been eliminated. For how long? For as long as you like ... for ever if you want. This does of course have implications for your original choice of reinforcer, it has to be sustainable in terms of time and cost.

Chapter 14:

Asking Green Questions, Answering Them, And Producing A **RAID**® Treatment Plan

***Red* questions focus on the extreme behaviour. For example:**

- What sanctions should we apply *when he hits someone?*

- What should we do *when he absconds?*

- What should we do when we catch him *stealing things?*

- What should we do when *she won't go to school?*

- What should we do when he keeps on *ripping up his clothes?*

***Green* Questions are ones that focus on good, adaptive, green behaviour**

- How can we get him to respect other people?

- How can we get him to stay on the unit?

- How can we get her to be more honest?

- How can we get her to want to go to school?

- How can we get him to wear clothes just like anyone else?

Ask green questions, not red ones.

Ask green questions, not red ones.

Thanks to our upbringing and training many people ask red questions, not green ones. This is a great pity because, usually, red questions lead nowhere productive. Take for example a typical question I was asked on a course:

What should we do when John, who is ten years old, comes out of his room in the middle of the night and starts smashing the place up, and assaults staff when they try to stop him?

What sort of an answer can you give to that question? Teach the staff a new wrist lock? Call for more staff to overpower John? Hardly very productive interventions.

Ask a green question, however, and all sorts of possibilities open up. A green question in this instance might be:

How can we get John to sleep through the night?

Green questions have two defining characteristics:

• *They focus on good, adaptive behaviour rather than the extreme behaviour*

• *If we can answer the green question, the extreme behaviour is overcome*

Hence a question such as 'Why does he wake up in the night and assault staff' is a red one on both counts. Firstly it talks about the extreme behaviour (waking up and assaulting staff) and, even if we could answer it, it would not resolve the extreme behaviour. For example the answer to the 'Why' question might be 'because he was sexually abused in his bedroom at the age of seven'. This answer does not resolve the current behaviour at all and in any event there would be no way of verifying such an answer.

EXERCISE

 One of the reasons we balk at asking green questions is a fear that we may not be able to answer them. They seem very 'global', too simple and yet too difficult. For example, try answering the question:

- *How can we get John, who is ten years old, to sleep through the night?*

Write as many good ideas as you can, here:

_____

_____

_____

_____

_____

_____

_____

_____

_____

_____

_____

Then turn over

You might have included some of these:

1. *Make sure he has a full, active day. Ensure he doesn't sleep during the day.*
2. *Check on his bed-time, make sure we are asking him to go to bed when he tired, not too early.*
3. *When he gets into bed, go and chat to him or read him a story - reinforce green behaviour in other words.*
4. *Make sure he hasn't has any caffeine-rich drinks in the evening ... coffee, tea, cola drinks.*
5. *Get him a bed-time routine that helps him wind down and relax.*
6. *Maybe give him a milky drink at bed-time.*
7. *Make sure he goes to the loo before bed, so he is less likely to be woken by a full bladder.*
8. *When he is lying in bed waiting to go to sleep - and when he has gone to sleep - pop in and check he is okay, not lonely.*
9. *Make sure any arguments are resolved before bed-time.*
10. *Ask him what might help him sleep through the night, maybe sharing a room with someone he likes if he is on his own, or maybe having a room on his own if he is sharing.*
11. *Give him some sort of reward or recognition when he sleeps through the night; or even just have a feed-back chart, one on which he can see how well he is doing.*
12. *Try and get his room so he is happy being in it; maybe a night-light, colours he likes, a radio with a timer which switches itself off after a bit, a cuddly toy if he wants one, even a TV if we can afford one.*

If you got even half of these, you would probably have resolved the extreme behaviour, as happened in real life.

But it may still be that you feel a little dissatisfied, cheated almost. Why should that be? Many people, perhaps all of us to a greater or lesser extent, suffer from the 'teach him a lesson' syndrome. *'If he's going to behave bad, then I'll show him who's boss.'*

But never mind, we have to learn to live with simply producing a radical solution that benefits everybody!

EXERCISE:

Below are four examples of Red questions and Green questions (non-productive questions and productive ones). Read through them, then fill in your own example in the space provided. Try to make your example relevant to someone you are working with currently.

Red Question: What can we do with him when he loses his temper?

Green Question: **How can we teach him to control his temper?**

Red Question: What should we do when she keeps pestering for tea and coffee all day long?

Green Question: **How can we get her to occupy herself constructively in the day, and just to have tea and coffee when the others do?**

Red Question: What do we do when he refuses to go to work / school?

Green Question?   **How can we get him to go to work / school?**

Red Question: How can we stop her stealing from the others?

Green Question: **How can we get her to be honest and respect others' property?**

Red Question:

Green Question:

EXERCISE:

Think of the people you work with (or even the people you live with!) and write down four green questions below. Remember, green questions have two defining characteristics:

- They focus on good, adaptive behaviour rather than the extreme behaviour

- If we can answer the green question, the extreme behaviour is overcome

So your green question will not contain the word 'not', nor the word 'why'. Either of these ensure that you go on to mention the red behaviour!

1.

2.

3.

4.

<u>ANSWERING</u> GREEN QUESTIONS:

THERE ARE SEVERAL STEPS

1. **Get a piece of paper and a pen.**

2. **Write your green question at the top of the paper. Check it really is green according to the criteria above.**

3. **Switch off your intelligence, we do not want the problem-solving, analytical part of your brain.**

4. **Below your green question write *any* possible answers that occur to you. Keep your pen moving, write anything you like. Don't worry if some of what you write seems to be crazy (that's why you're doing it on a separate piece of paper and not in this book … you can throw it away afterwards!)**

5. **When you run out of ideas, still think of some more, really dredge the resources of your mind. Some of the best ideas come at this stage.**

6. **When you are convinced that you cannot think of another answer, start analysing what you have written. Only now do you switch back on your logical mind.**

7. **Cross out any ideas that are completely lacking in feasibility. But beware, sometimes some apparently bizarre ideas have a grain of truth which is key to a really good solution.[4]**

8. **Finally, get a new piece of paper and summarise the good ideas so that you have a list something like we achieved for 'sleeping through the night'. This is your RAID treatment plan!**

---

[4] I was once asked for advice by a top-flight football team whose home record was second-to-none, but who had failed to win a single away match. The green question was 'How Can We Win Away Matches.' One of the fifty answers that were produced was 'get another team of players'. The logical mind would have scoffed at this because the existing players were winning at home so they must be skilled enough. It turned out that there was one player who was extremely bad for morale over the extended time of an away trip, though not at home because he simply turned up, played and went home again. The answer involved this player being left out of the away matches. This is an example of how the logical mind can lead us astray if we are not careful.

EXERCISE ON ANSWERING A GREEN QUESTION

Write your green question here. This may be taken from the previous exercise.

_____

_____

In the space below write as many possible answers as you can. Remember it does not matter if you include bizarre ones, you can evaluate them later. Use the facing page as well if you need to.

_____

_____

_____

_____

_____

_____

_____

_____

_____

_____

_____

_____

_____

THEN TURN TO THE NEXT PAGE FOR THE NEXT PART OF THE EXERCISE

Now switch back on the logical side of your brain and write down a feasible plan of action to answer the green question that you started with:

_____

_____

_____

_____

_____

_____

_____

_____

_____

_____

_____

_____

_____

_____

_____

_____

_____

_____

_____

_____

Chapter 15:

Getting The Person To Look Towards The Future (That Means Putting More Green Into The Funnel)

In our RAID model, looking to the future is equivalent to putting green fluid in the funnel. Remember, the syringe represents the client, and the funnel and tube represents our intervention. The green fluid in the funnel is not yet into the person, but it is on its way. In other words, it is the future.

'The Future' means very different things for different people. For you, reading this, you may think of the future as six months from now, a year from now, even five or ten years from now. Other people may have trouble seeing as far ahead as the next meal time, or even what they are going to do when they reach the chair they are walking towards. Even so, all these represent the future, and are all important for the individual concerned.

Why is the future so important?

The future is important for two reasons. In terms of 'pure' extreme behaviour, it is largely consideration of the future that keeps us 'on track' in the present. After all, why do you continue to go into work? Is it because you can think of nothing more pleasurable to do? Or is it maybe because you can see into the future and wish to continue paying your rent or mortgage, maybe buy a more sophisticated hi-fi, want to continue going out to the cinema on Saturday evenings, and have your eye on a more up-market car? Equally, others are kept on track still by envisaging the future, but a negative version they wish to avoid. This is fine too, and such people would continue to go to work because they do not want their house repossessed, they don't want their car (being bought on payments) taken back, and so on.

And the same principle holds good right across the board. If Alan is busy thinking about what he is going to buy in town when he gets there, he is less likely to respond aggressively to Bertie winding him up. If Chris is totally obsessed with his ambition to become a gardener, his thoughts of burglary gradually diminish to the back of his mind, and the sanction of maybe ending up in prison becomes very much more meaningful because it would interfere with his cherished dream. If Dave is looking forward to seeing a particular video this evening he is less likely to be concerned with smashing the place up this afternoon.

The other major reason for looking to the future is somewhat more gloomy. Staggeringly, in the U.K. suicide is the third largest cause of lost years of life. One of the major factors in suicide is so-called 'hopelessness'. That is, a lack of hope for the future. Put another way, many people are unable to envisage an attractive future. If they could, then maybe they would stay around to try and achieve it.

So how do we do it?
(get people to envisage and work towards the future, that is).

We are talking about two different things here, aren't we. The first is how we get people to envisage the future, which requires ingenuity. The second is how we get them to work towards it, which draws on our personal qualities and perseverance.

Getting people to envisage the future can be done casually or formally. Casually, we can simply ask questions which invite the person to look future-wards. Questions like:

> *'What are you going to have in the drinks-break?'*
>
> *'What do you think there will be for lunch?'*
>
> *'What do you want to buy when we go to town this afternoon?'*
>
> *'What shall we do this evening?'*
>
> *'What are you going to do tomorrow?'*
>
> *'What shall we do at the weekend?'*
>
> *'What are you going to do in the holidays?'*
>
> *'What shall we do at Christmas?'*
>
> *'What would you like to be doing a year from now?'*
>
> *'What would you like to be doing five years from now?'*

Clearly, not all of these are green for all people. Equally, we have to be careful when we ask such questions, and in what tone of voice do so. People are generally more responsive to these sort of questions when they are already relaxed and already thinking about things. In other words, when the question is 'in context'. If we just spring such questions onto people we are likely to be rebuffed pretty smartly. Pictures can be useful, too. I think it is no accident that we tend to use the word 'picture' in sentences such *'I can picture exactly where I'd like to be in 1 year's time.'*

So if we can literally draw out people's plans for them then I believe this is a big step forward. Or, better still, if we can get them to draw the pictures for themselves.

Sometimes we can use a combination of graphics and words. One of my favourites is the ladder. In this you literally draw a ladder and put at the top of it whatever the person wants to achieve. This is crucial, whatever goes at the top <u>must come from the person</u> and not you.

Once you have that crucial item at the top, something that the person really wants to achieve, then we can fill in (with the person) the steps necessary to achieve whatever it is they want. This is why it is so crucial that what's at the top of the ladder has come from them. If they don't really want what's at the top, then the steps are also meaningless.

So, an example might be like this:

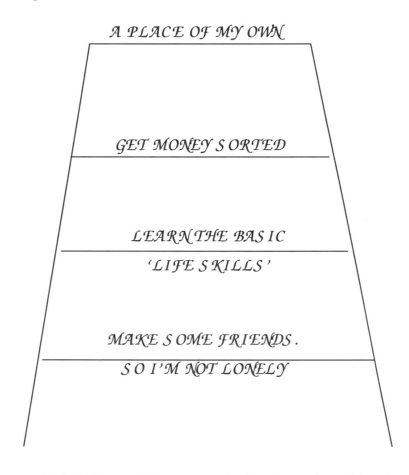

Other examples can include boats sailing past particular islands, intrepid explorers climbing up hills and mountains representing particular life-difficulties, and so on.

So far, then, we have been talking about *illustrating* what a person wants to do. But pictures can also be used to *instruct* a person what should be done. This still concerns the future, it is still describing what green behaviour is, but simply leading it on future-wards. An example might be the cartoon strip on the side of this page which illustrates an early-morning routine. This not only describes what green behaviour is, it enables the person to literally see what should come next.

Just by the way, it is interesting that some people regard pictures and visual aids as 'low level'. I am not convinced of this at all. Sure, they may be used with clients who have a relatively low level of intellectual functioning, but equally, I think they are stunningly useful right across the board. As an experiment, why don't you try out the ladder technique for yourself. Draw a ladder, put on top of it something you really want, and write in the necessary steps on the rungs. Actually, come to think of it, I will draw one for you, just to make it easy:

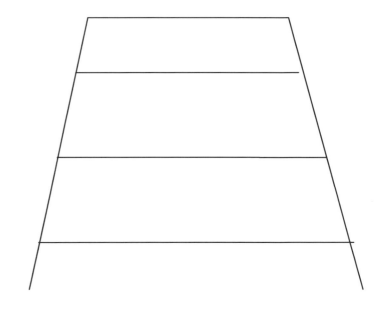

There are also some *activities* which lead a person

to think of the future. Gardening must be the prime example. Personally, I do almost no gardening, but I think it must be a mistake because all the evidence shows that it is a terrific activity. It is no wonder that at one time, many of the psychiatric hospitals had farms and gardens. A great shame they have virtually disappeared. The beauty of such activity is not just that there is some kind of basic satisfaction in interacting with nature but also that it automatically cues people in towards the future. Without any instruction people start anticipating what the seed they have sown will look like, or the bulbs, or the potatoes, or whatever. Some very optimistic gardeners may be literally unable to wait until tomorrow to see what progress their fledgling plants have made.

Likewise, some serials and soap operas (Coronation Street, Eastenders, and so on) have a similar effect. Viewers literally "look forward" to what is going to happen.

In summary, we can:

- Ask questions which get a person thinking of the future

- Draw pictures which record the person's plans for the future[5]

- We can draw pictures to communicate how the future will pan out, getting up out of bed, having breakfast, and so on.

- We can indulge in activities such as gardening and watching serials which invite the person to think of the future.

Achieving the future

Occasionally we get so wrapped up in sophisticated techniques that the simple art of encouraging and supporting our clients is forgotten. Yet we all know that such support, given enthusiastically and warmly, is often quite invaluable and overrides many a technique.

If we want outside support for such a view, we can look to three authors. Mischel, in 1973, pointed out that people will not carry out a task, *even if they anticipate reward,* if they don't expect themselves to be successful in it. Bandura, in 1989, made out the case that *a history of past success* is one of the things that makes a client believe in their ability to succeed. However, many clients do not necessarily have a history of past success, and it is Baron, in 1988, who highlights eloquently the importance of *encouragement and support* to overcome that fact.

---

[5] Interestingly, almost all organisations have 'wall charts' to depict their plans for the future. To try replacing these by a verbal account, or a simple list of what should happen, would cause havoc!

It is not sufficient simply to help the client plan out their future and then tell them to get on with achieving it. Most clients will need a great deal of support and encouragement if they are to succeed. Support in overcoming all the myriad of hurdles that appear, or in reviewing the life plan if their goals turn out to be unachievable.

CHAPTER 16:

What To Do If You Can Work Out What He Or She Is Getting Out Of Behaving Red

So far we have concentrated almost entirely on the green behaviour. How to set things up to elicit more green behaviour, how to ask – and answer – green questions, and so on. Let's now look at the red behaviour and see whether it too can give us some clues about how we can work against it.

One of the questions I hear most often is 'Why does he do it?' – 'it' referring to whatever the extreme behaviour is. There are some good 'Why' questions and some bad ones. Or, more to the point, there are some good *answers* and some bad ones. The bad answers can sometimes sound good, providing some exotic explanation for the reason behind it, but ultimately falling down on two grounds: (1) the explanation cannot be verified and (2) the explanation doesn't lead to any useful intervention. Good answers on the other hand are the reverse: the answer can be verified, and they lead to a useful intervention.

Answers of this sort usually centre around two things: (a) what the person is achieving by behaving extremely – 'what they are getting out of it', and (b) what triggers the extreme behaviour – <u>when</u> it happens.

Let's look at each in turn. First, what the person is achieving by behaving extremely, 'what they are getting out of it', sometimes summarised as the 'function' of the behaviour.

On the next page are some examples of extreme behaviours I have come across, and their functions in those particular cases. I should emphasise that even if one of the people who you work with shows just the same behaviour it does not necessarily mean it serves the same function. (We will look at how to decide that, later on.)

Examples of extreme behaviour and its function

Example 1: A man of 30 years old, with severe learning disabilities, nearly blind and nearly deaf. His extreme behaviour was that he was scratching his face and head to the extent that he now had open wounds on both. The function of the behaviour turned out to be to obtain sensory stimulation.

Example 2: A fifteen-year-old girl with no particular pathology. Her extreme behaviour was sulking. Frequently and for a long time. The function turned out to be to express her anger.

Example 3: A sixteen-year-old girl living in a residential home. Her extreme behaviour was to lie in bed all day every day. The function turned out to be to avoid the feeling of loneliness (when she was up and about the others in the home shunned her; this wasn't so apparent to her so long as she stayed in bed).

Example 4: A 32-year-old man in a secure facility whose extreme behaviour is to self-harm by cutting himself. It turns out that this is a very effective way for him to reduce the feelings of tension he gets, so that is its function.

Example 5: Is a 41-year-old man with a history of attacking females and sexually assaulting them. In his case it turns out that this was to achieve sexual gratification. Although this motive sounds an obvious one, it is not always the case that sexual attacks are for sexual gratification.

Now try the exercise on the next page.

Individual Exercise

Think of one of the people you work with, and write down a further example of a specific challenging behaviour and its function.

The person:

_R T._

The extreme behaviour (if he or she produces more than one type of extreme behaviour, choose just one):

Screaming + Shouting

Your best guess as to the function of the extreme behaviour (don't worry for the moment that it is just a guess at this point):

to get hold attention

So what now?

Let's assume you have mad a pretty good guess as to the function of your person's extreme behaviour, what should you do now? The answer is simple: you <u>help the person achieve that function in a green way</u> – a better way, a way that is more effective for him or her and does not involve the use of any extreme behaviour.

Although this answer seems fairly obvious (I hope) it is not what often happens in practice. Frequently I see the function put down as 'attention-seeking' and the action taken as 'ensuring he doesn't get attention when he does the extreme behaviour'. Needless to say, this very rarely works.

So what we should do is to:
- ♣ help the scratcher to get sensory stimulation in a better way
- ♣ help the sulker express their anger assertively and openly
- ♣ help the self-harmer to relieve tension some other way
- ♣ etc.

Individual Exercise

Consider the example you produced overleaf. How could you help the person achieve the same function in a better way? Write down any ideas you have, right now:

_____

_____

_____

_____

_____

_____

In summary ...

*"Challenging Behaviour is not the problem but the solution.
The real problem is finding a better solution."*

Thoreau

CHAPTER 17:

What To Do If You Can Work Out What is Triggering the Red Behaviour

We have seen from the previous chapter that it can sometimes be useful to examine the functions of extreme behaviour. Although it seems when we do that we are losing our focus on green behaviour, we regain that focus by later asking what green ways the person can achieve the function they are after.

In the same way it can sometimes be useful to look what *triggers* an episode of challenging behaviour.

For example:

Example 1: Ben's habit of attacking Alan is triggered by Alan winding him up.

Example 2: Equally, Alan's habit of winding up Ben is triggered by Alan's boredom. He tends to do it much less when he is involved in something he is interested in.

Example 3: Hanna's habit of getting into fights with other residents is triggered by queuing for meals. Over the last month, three quarters of the fights that Hanna has been in have taken place in meal queues.

Example 4: The self harm referred to in the example in the previous chapter could be said to be triggered by the tension felt by the man.

Example 5: Dave's verbal abuse to staff in the residential home in which he lived was triggered by visits from his brother. Both before and after his brother visiting him, Dave was liable to be abusive.

Example 6: Elaine's screaming was triggered by the word 'No' (when she asked staff for something) or, sometimes, simply be being refused whatever she wanted (no matter how gently it was put).

Now try the exercise on the next page.

Exercise

Think of the same person as in the previous chapter, and the same behaviour. But this time, instead of specifying its function, specify its trigger.

The person:

_____

_____

_____

_____

The extreme behaviour (if he or she produces more than one type of extreme behaviour, choose just one):

_____

_____

_____

_____

Your best guess as to the trigger of the extreme behaviour (don't worry for the moment that it is just a guess at this point). Write more than one trigger if you want:

_____

_____

_____

_____

So, assuming we have identified the trigger, what should we do?

We have 3 options: we can either:

¬ **Remove (or 'spoil') the trigger,** *or*
¬ **Teach the person to cope with the trigger,**   *or*
¬ **Spot the trigger occurring without the challenging behaviour and immediately reinforce**

So, We Might
- ♣ Separate Alan from Ben, because Alan's winding up is the trigger for Ben's attack, *or*
- ♣ Teach Ben how to cope with being wound up, e.g. walking away, *or*
- ♣ Spot times when Alan winds up Ben, but Ben walks away, and reinforce that.

Or, if Alan's habit of winding up Ben is triggered by Alan's boredom, we might
- ♣ Keep Alan occupied
- ♣ Teach Alan how to cope when he is bored; how to occupy himself
- ♣ Spot times when – in spite of being bored – Alan is not winding up Ben, and reinforce those times

Or, if tension were the trigger for Chris's self-harm we might:
- ♣ Help Chris lead a low-tension life, *or*
- ♣ Help Chris cope with the tension another way, e.g. come and talk to us, *or*
- ♣ Spot Chris being tense but not harming herself, and reinforce.

Or, if Dave's verbal abuse follows a visit from relatives we might:
- ♣ 'Spoil' the trigger by sitting in on the visits, *or*
- ♣ Help Dave cope with the effect his relatives have on him, *or*
- ♣ Notice times when relatives have visited but Dave has shown little or no verbal abuse, and reinforce

Or, if Hanna's fights are triggered by queuing for meals, we might:
- ♣ Remove the trigger by introducing a different meals system
- ♣ Help Hanna cope with the trigger by teaching her how to occupy herself in a queue
- ♣ Notice when when Hanna seems calm when queuing, and reinforce those times.

Now try the exercise on the next page...

Individual Exercise,

Using your own example of challenging behaviour and its trigger, what intervention would you make? You might like to see what each option looks like, for your example:

'Removing or spoiling the trigger' in this case would mean:

_____

_____

_____

_____

'Help the person cope with the trigger' in this case would mean:

_____

_____

_____

_____

'Spot the trigger occurring without the challenging behaviour and immediately reinforce' in this case would mean:

_____

_____

_____

_____

Finally, try the exercise on the next page: think of the same client, and decide for yourself whether it most useful to consider the functions of the behaviour, or its triggers

 EXERCISE

Functions and Triggers

Name _____

Extreme Behaviour _____

Function(s) of extreme behaviour[1] _____

_____

Trigger for extreme behaviour[2] _____

_____

_____

Chosen intervention _____

_____

_____

[1] An intervention based on having determined the function(s) of the extreme behaviour normally provides a Green way for the person to achieve the specified function(s).

[2] An intervention based on having determined the trigger(s) of the extreme behaviour, normally will rely on one or more of the following:
♦ Removing or spoiling the trigger.
♦ Teaching the person to cope with the occurrence of the trigger in a Green way.
♦ Noticing the trigger occurring, but no ensuing extreme behaviour and reinforcing that behaviour.

CHAPTER 18:

Working Out What Function Is Served By Behaving Red

and

Working Out What Is Triggering The Red Behaviour

In the previous two chapters we talked as though you already knew the function and the triggers of the extreme behaviour. And maybe you do; very often we have a very perceptive notion of just what underlies the behaviour. Equally, however, we can sometimes be badly mistaken, being quite certain we know what underlies it but, when real data comes in, being quite wrong.

So, in this chapter we are going to look at two ways of achieving a functional analysis (working out what the function of the behaviour is, and what its triggers are). One way is normally reckoned to be 'the right way', the other is a much more RAIDing way.

The 'right way' first. This is easy enough: you simply fill in the forms overleaf (you can photocopy as many of them as you want) and then you analyse them. Several points to be made, however:

- A number of forms - <u>focussing on one client, and just one specific extreme behaviour</u> - should be completed before attempting any analysis.
- During the completion of the forms we should <u>keep a completely open mind</u> as to what the analysis will reveal, so we record just what a camera and microphone might record.
- We <u>use clear, unambiguous terms</u>, eg: *'Jo punched Fred on the ear'* rather than *'Jo expressed his/her aggression towards Fred.'*

The RAID® functional analysis form

An account of extreme behaviour from (client) _____

The behaviour:

What did he/she do? *This is the "extreme behaviour". Be as specific as you can.*

_____

_____

The circumstances:

What was the time, day and date? _____

Where was s/he? _____

What was s/he doing *and about to do*?

_____

What were others doing *and about to do*?

_____

The antecedents:

Where had s/he just come from, if anywhere? _____

What had s/he just been doing, and been doing some time before?

_____

What had relevant others been doing, and been doing some time before?

_____

The result:

What *actually* happened after the behaviour in question (maybe as a result of it, maybe not.) Include what happened immediately, and what happened longer term.

_____

_____

The RAID® functional analysis form

An account of extreme behaviour from (client) _____

The behaviour:

What did he/she do? *This is the "extreme behaviour". Be as specific as you can.*

_____

_____

The circumstances:

What was the time, day and date? _____

Where was s/he? _____

What was s/he doing *and about to do*?

_____

What were others doing *and about to do*?

_____

The antecedents:

Where had s/he just come from, if anywhere? _____

What had s/he just been doing, and been doing some time before?

_____

What had relevant others been doing, and been doing some time before?

_____

The result:

What *actually* happened after the behaviour in question (maybe as a result of it, maybe not.) Include what happened immediately, and what happened longer term.

_____

_____

This form may be copied freely

Analysing the forms:

Once you have a reasonable number of forms, then is the time for analysis. What 'a reasonable number' is, will depend on the particular extreme behaviour. The main point to remember is:

All the forms we analyse must be for
♣ **the same person, and**
♣ **the same extreme behaviour.**

So if Jo exhibits three different extreme behaviours, eg (i) hitting people, (ii) spitting, (iii) pestering staff, we have a pile of RAID forms relating just to Jo hitting people. We leave spitting and pestering to one side until later.

As for the analysis itself, we look for a clear pattern. This pattern might be any of the following:

♣ A regular event that has happened before the occurrence of extreme behaviour, eg being visited by a parent, being 'told off', or being 'wound up'.
♣ A regular activity during which it takes place, eg queuing for meals, or during woodwork sessions.
♣ Shortly before specific activities, eg just before going to bed, or before outings.
♣ It might even be that the extreme behaviour is being inadvertently encouraged by what happens after it, eg a caring staff member always sitting the person down and having a 1:1 chat over a cup of tea.

One or two more important points

♣ A trigger does not have to be on <u>every</u> form. 60% will do. Likewise function. This is because an extreme behaviour may have <u>several</u> triggers, or serve any of several functions.
♣ Some functions/triggers are obscure, eg 'boredom' (nothing happening) or 'frustration' (several possible causes). These are difficult – but not impossible – to uncover.

Next: A RAIDing alternative to a true functional analysis

At the beginning of the chapter I said that we would look at two ways of establishing what are the functions and triggers of an extreme behaviour. This second way is not a true functional analysis, but it is good nevertheless. In some ways better than what we have just covered.

The problems with the form-filling methods are twofold:

1. Some people – sometimes including those who know the patient / client / person best – have little or no patience with form-filling
2. What happens if the extreme behaviour is very damaging to others – a serious physical assault, say – can we really wait for half a dozen such episodes to take place, so that we can collect our forms? Probably not.

So what is the alternative? Ask yourself (with conviction) the following question:

If there were £1 million in it for me, what would I do to prevent Ken's extreme behaviour for the next 2 days?

Your Answers Might Include:
- ♣ Keep him busy, or
- ♣ Let him sit quietly by himself, or
- ♣ Make sure his brother doesn't visit, or
- ♣ Make sure he has plenty of drink, or
- ♣ Have John spend plenty of time talking to him
- ♣ Make sure we've got plenty of videotapes in
- ♣ Keep Sue away from him
- ♣ etc

And remember, all of these may be true, because an extreme behaviour often – usually even – has more than one function or trigger.

But the answers given above, although they have obvious relevance, don't immediately tell us what the functions of and triggers for Ken's behaviour are. We cannot yet connect with the material in the previous two chapters, which told us what to do when we know what the functions and triggers are.

So there is an intervening step, as described in the exercise on the next page...

Exercise

The following suggestions were made for preventing Ken's behaviour:

- ♣ Keep him busy, or
- ♣ Let him sit quietly by himself, or
- ♣ Make sure his brother doesn't visit, or
- ♣ Make sure he has plenty of drink, or
- ♣ Have John spend plenty of time talking to him
- ♣ Make sure we've got plenty of videotapes in
- ♣ Keep Sue away from him

Please answer the following questions on the functions and triggers revealed by those suggestions. The first two have been done for you.

Tip: Often, an extreme behaviour is a form of communication, trying to tell us something.

Tip 2: Sometimes an extreme behaviour may have a trigger, but no obvious function, or vice versa.

1) What function or trigger for Ken's extreme behaviour is suggested by the fact that 'keeping him busy' may prevent that behaviour?

Function: to alleviate boredom / provide him with interest

Trigger: Boredom

2) What function or trigger for Ken's extreme behaviour is suggested by the fact that 'letting him sit quietly by himself' may prevent that behaviour?

Function: to get others to leave him alone

Trigger: Being hassled / over-stimulated

3) What function or trigger for Ken's extreme behaviour is suggested by the fact that 'Making sure his brother doesn't visit' may prevent that behaviour?

Function: _____

Trigger: _____

4) What function or trigger for Ken's extreme behaviour is suggested by the fact that 'Make sure he has plenty of drink' may prevent that behaviour?

Function: _____

Trigger: _____

5) What function or trigger for Ken's extreme behaviour is suggested by the fact that 'Have John spend plenty of time talking to him' may prevent that behaviour?

Function: _____

Trigger: _____

6) What function or trigger for Ken's extreme behaviour is suggested by the fact that 'Make sure we've got plenty of videotapes in' may prevent that behaviour?

Function: _____

Trigger: _____

7) What function or trigger for Ken's extreme behaviour is suggested by the fact that 'Keep Sue away from him' may prevent that behaviour?

Function: _____

Trigger: _____

Mini Exercise:

You have probably been thinking of someone you are working with, while doing this exercise. What implications has the content of this chapter and the two preceding ones got for your work with that person?

_____

_____

_____

_____

CHAPTER 19:
Some sort of a summary

You could look at it that there are three 'bins' we can aim to dump the extreme behaviour into:

BIN 1: is for extreme behaviour which really does not seem to serve any useful purpose for the person displaying it, and doesn't even seem to be sparked off by anything in particular. This is the one we have been talking about in most of the book, up until the last couple of chapter.

BIN 2: is for extreme behaviour that seems to serve some sort of function. For example where a resident pinches others to show s/he wants some 'space' or privacy, or where youngsters wind up others to alleviate boredom.

- To dump extreme behaviour in this bin we can do as for Bin 1, but also work out how to achieve that same function in a better way. For example, to help the first person to indicate when they want privacy by saying or signing; to try to provide the second person with a more stimulating routine.*

BIN 3: is for behaviour which we can see has been sparked off by something in particular. For example Jo might be in the habit of assaulting others when he has been wound up by one of his contemporaries; Sue might assault others when she is kept waiting for something she wants. To dump extreme behaviour in this bin we have to choose; either we can:

- alter the situation. Maybe it is the case that Sue is kept waiting for unreasonable lengths of time, in which case we need to address that.
OR
- teach new ways of coping. For example we might teach Jo to count to ten, or to walk away, or whatever seems best.
OR
- spot times when they don't display the extreme behaviour even though the 'trigger' is there, and reinforce their *actual* behaviour. (For example we might notice that Jo was wound up by one of his contemporaries, but did not assault anyone; we would want to reinforce this.)

If you cannot decide between the 3 bins, go for bin 1! Why not try the exercise you did earlier, to see if you want to use just Bin 1 (under 'chosen intervention'). There's another copy of it on the next page.

 EXERCISE

Functions and Triggers

Name _____

Extreme Behaviour _____

Function(s) of extreme behaviour[1] _____

_____

Trigger for extreme behaviour[2] _____

_____

_____

Chosen intervention _____

_____

_____

[1] An intervention based on having determined the function(s) of the extreme behaviour normally provides a Green way for the person to achieve the specified function(s).

[2] An intervention based on having determined the trigger(s) of the extreme behaviour, normally will rely on one or more of the following:
♦ Removing or spoiling the trigger.
♦ Teaching the person to cope with the occurrence of the trigger in a Green way.
♦ Noticing the trigger occurring, but no ensuing extreme behaviour and reinforcing that behaviour.

Section Three:

RAIDing at the moment of extreme behaviour

Chapter 20:

What to do when Red behaviour happens:

Option 1, Ignore it.

In this and the next few chapters I want us to have a look at the options you have when red behaviour happens. You should regard the options as a 'menu', each of the items on the menu is fine in itself, but it is a matter of you choosing the best one. The items on the menu are:

- ♣ **Literally ignore the red behaviour**
- ♣ **Minimal intervention: do what has to be done, but in a low key way**
- ♣ **Address the issue, probably not at the moment of red behaviour, but later on**
- ♣ **Give feedback**
- ♣ **Benign punishment, some consequence designed to discourage the behaviour but benefit the person**
- ♣ **Sanctions, penalties that have to be imposed**

In this chapter we look at the role of *literally ignoring* the extreme behaviour.

The real learning and development of individuals takes place when they behave 'right' rather than 'wrong', so long as we make sure we respond to that 'right' behaviour. So, although we feel as though we must 'get in quick' when extreme behaviour occurs, this is not really the case; we can often ignore it or play it down. We actually need to get in quick when *adaptive* behaviour occurs; Reinforcing Appropriate.

So when might we be right to literally ignore some extreme behaviour?

Some examples:

Example 1, is a foster carer who found herself increasingly losing patience with the 13-year-old girl she was looking after. The 13-year-old, Ingrid, seemed intent on 'picking a fight with' Joanne, the foster-carer. She had a range of strategies for doing this, chief amongst which was that she would criticise Joanne for various perceived misdemeanours. For instance, she said 'You promised we would go to town after school today,' when in fact Joanne had not promised, merely casually agreed that it might be a nice thing to do.

Typically Joanne would react to this by arguing about whether it had been a promise or a comment, both would dig in their heels that their perception was the correct one, and it would end up with one or both of them storming off and remaining angry and bitter for hours or days.

On the basis of the 'it takes two to tango' reasoning, Joanne decided to actively ignore these attempts at picking a fight and, after a few false starts, managed to perfect her technique. She referred to it as the 'Columbo technique' – acting as though she was so dumb or in such a good mood that she didn't realise that Ingrid was trying to pick a fight with her. She reported that the result was little short of a transformation. She was particularly struck that Ingrid herself seemed grateful for the new strategy. Although she never said so openly, Joanne perceived that she appeared grateful that 'a moments madness' was not responded to, and therefore did not lead on to hours or days of unhappiness.

Example 2 involved the same principle but rather more distressing behaviour. Ken was a compulsorily detained patient in a secure facility. He suffered from schizophrenia, which was only partially controlled by anti-psychotic medication, and one of his extreme behaviours was to smear and throw excrement. There was some debate amongst the multidisciplinary team as to the extent that Ken knew what he was doing. On the one hand there were times when he was 'on a good level'; at those times it was difficult to believe he would indulge in such behaviours. But at other times he seemed to 'deliberately' target certain staff. Not unreasonably, those staff – and indeed their colleagues – took a dim view of this.

The result was that 'sanctions' were applied and Ken would lose out until – usually – he ended up in a bare room with no clothes and just a foam rubber mattress to sleep on. And yet still he would be smearing and throwing excrement. In fact, some staff believed that he did it more when sanctions were applied.

Ken led to protracted and heart-searching discussions, and eventually it was felt that – although unwittingly – Ken was actually 'setting the agenda'. In other words, Ken's treatment seemed to be dictated by Ken's actions rather than the principles of the team. It was therefore decided to ignore his behaviour as far as possible, simply getting him to clean things up if possible and, if not, to have someone else clean it up. Also, as much as reasonably could be was allowed into Ken's room. At the same time the principle of 'the more rewarding the life, the less the extreme behaviour' was applied, and every effort was made to make his life more rewarding. One of the main methods was to have a couple of the staff he seemed to get on with spend more time talking to him, and to take him out on short walks when he was on good form.

The decision was also taken – importantly – to monitor the frequency of Ken's smearing and throwing both before and after the new policy. Overall there was a reduction of around 65% - his smearing and throwing reduced to about one third of its previous level. It was important that this monitoring was done because Ken's extreme behaviour, although only one third of what it had been, was still very distressing to staff. It was therefore very important for all of us to know that the new policy was being effective.

So ignoring red behaviour can be the best option, so long as – at the same time - every effort is made to introduce and reinforce green behaviour. Nevertheless there are times when you cannot ignore red behaviour. The three main occasions are:

1. *When the safety of the client or others is in jeopardy.*
   This situation speaks for itself; whatever the long-term effects, there are occasions where one simply has to intervene for the safety and well-being of the client or others.

2. *When the client's behaviour demands some form of sanction.*
   There are times when we may judge that, even though the client's best interests may be served by our ignoring a behaviour, or intervening in a minimal fashion, his or her behaviour was so extreme that it demands a more substantial intervention. The usual reason for this is to express public disapproval for the action in question, and to establish in the minds of others that the behaviour is not acceptable.

   An example of this was the judge who imposed a £500 fine on a young man who had raped a fifteen year old girl, on the grounds that a custodial sentence would in no way benefit the client. In that respect he may have been right, but public opinion demanded a more severe penalty, and a custodial sentence was handed down on appeal. Similar situations happen on a smaller domestic or residential scale.

   Note: This heading *'When the client's behaviour demands some form of sanction* is a dangerous one for us because, when we are having a bad day, almost anything that anybody does demands some form of sanction. Clearly this puts at risk the whole RAID philosophy we have built up. We must therefore (a) keep the RAID acronym to the front of the mind, this sub-head at the back, and (b) do all we can to minimise the number of bad days we have!

3. *When the client's behaviour is intrinsically reinforcing.* For example: public masturbation, some instances of head-banging. Plainly, if you simply ignore a behaviour that is enjoyable in its own right, it will continue. In that case we have to redress the balance in some way, to provide some dis-incentive to continue that behaviour.

In summary then, ignoring – the first item on our menu – can be an good and effective strategy even in some very severe behaviours, so long as we remember that our main task is to generate and reinforce green behaviour in people. Equally, there is some behaviour that certainly cannot be ignored. Our wisdom in differentiating the one from the other will be an important factor in our success.

Chapter 21:

What to do when Red behaviour happens:

Option 2, Minimal Intervention

In practice, minimal intervention is only slightly different from 'ignoring'. You might think of it as 'doing what has to be done, but ignoring it in your heart'.

So,
- ♣ **If Alan and Ben are fighting with each other, you separate them.**
- ♣ **If one youngster is saying or about to say something so vicious that it will psychologically damage the recipient for life, you stop him or her.**
- ♣ **If Ken is smearing faeces, you get it cleaned up.**
- ♣ **If a psychotic patient is walking around with no clothes on, or masturbating in public, you protect them.**
- ♣ **And so on. There is no implication that you necessarily need to do anything further at that moment. Why not? Because you have in place your master plan that will generate and reinforce green behaviour long-term, thereby overwhelming the red behaviour eventually.**

Case Study 1:

Two residents in a home for people moving from a psychiatric hospital to the community were in the habit of bickering with each other. This tended to be quite disruptive as often it took place when others were trying to watch the TV.

One or two of the staff members became quite skilled at deflecting the two residents involved, usually by taking them into another room to play a board game, or, on other occasions, to get a drink.

The problem with this approach was that, although it solved the immediate problem, it also rewarded these incidents of bickering and made them more likely to recur. This was indeed what had happened.

It was decided that it was not feasible to *totally* ignore the bickering, because it was so disruptive to others. A minimal intervention strategy was therefore adopted, where the two bickerers were instructed to leave the room, and were shepherded out if necessary. In this way the disruptive behaviour was all but ignored.

There was still the issue of why these two particular people tended to bicker with each other, and this was addressed as a separate matter, when neither was behaving disruptively. Previously, there had been a tendency to address this immediately, sometimes whilst getting a drink. In that case, the conscientious staff members had unwittingly reinforced the bickering with (a) the drink, and (b) their undivided attention to sort out this relationship difficulty.

So it is fine to sort out the difficulty, but we do need to be wary about the exact *timing*.

Case-study 2:

Linda was a compulsorily-detained patient who was in the habit of cutting herself, especially when she felt tense. She would cut herself severely and frequently, and reported a great release in tension when she did so. You will know from our earlier discussion that our long-term plan was to help Linda get the same release of tension in a green way – achieve the same function in a green way. (In this case mainly by learning to talk to certain staff and, later, friends, to obtain emotional support.)

Nevertheless, the question arose as to how to respond when Linda cut herself. One the one hand you don't want to encourage such behaviour, on the other hand you want to be supportive to someone who is in such distress that they cut themselves. So we intervened *as minimally as possible*. So, we dressed the wound if necessary. This is not to say, however, that we made a big fuss of the person, brew up a cup of tea, settle down for a long and sympathetic talk, and so on. Nevertheless we did dress the wounds in a mildly supportive way: minimal intervention.

A general note: Some people – quite rightly - are particularly interested in the *manner* in which they should dress the wounds of someone who has self-harmed. Should there perhaps be a faintly disapproving flavour to it? I think we find the answer by going back to *Why the RAID approach works*. Some of the important elements are:

- setting a good model, or a good example,
- building the person up, and
- maintaining a good relationship between the client and ourselves.

All these point us in the direction of being warm and sympathetic, but - because we do not want to encourage such behaviour - only faintly so. Probably the best analogy is to do with 'strokes' (a transactional analysis term): I would suggest that when a person harms themselves they do indeed receive a few positive strokes. We might feel that this encourages such behaviour, but the point is that - so long as we are working within a generally RAIDing service - there are easier and better ways of getting positive strokes, and in much larger quantities. We therefore don't need to worry that our patient will turn to self harm as the one and only way of getting attention from us.

In summary, there are a number of situations that we cannot literally ignore, we need to intervene in some way. Many of those involve the physical or emotional safety of the person we are looking after. In those situations we do not necessarily need to make a big event of the extreme behaviour. We do, however, unequivocally need to do what is necessary to safeguard the person. And, moreover, by virtue of the fact that we are now working in a RAIDing service, we can do so in a 'reasonable' way.

Chapter 22:

What to do when Red behaviour happens: Option 3, Feedback

Feedback is a very powerful concept indeed and might be defined as:

Giving information, in order to help someone to achieve clear goals.

In other words there are 3 distinct elements:

Giving information ... . Sometimes a professional will mistakenly turn feedback into a discussion. This is not necessary, and, if the feedback you are giving is negative, is likely to end in an argument. Better simply to give the information and hope that, either immediately or later, the person will respond to it.

... to help someone ... An important part of feedback. It is intended to be helpful, not to 'get at' the person concerned.

... to achieve clear goals... One of the most frequent reasons that a person takes no notice of our feedback is that it makes no link with their goals - sometimes because they simply have none! As we have said before, such an absence of a view of the future is bad news ... for the client and, probably, for those around him.

More on feedback

Feedback is used for two purposes:

1. As a reward (so it is not just something we can do when red behaviour happens, we can use it powerfully when green behaviour happens too).

2. To inform clients of what is right and wrong.

As a reward it can be very powerful indeed. If you bring to mind the nature of feedback - a straightforward appraisal of how a client has performed - this comes across as a very objective and non-manipulative social reward. Clients can therefore find statements from you such as 'You showed a lot of self-control there, not responding when X was trying to wind you up' as very positive and reinforcing. Equally, feedback is a powerful tool in enabling people to learn the difference between right and wrong. Frequently one hears statements such as 'If we use virtually no punishment, how do clients ever learn the difference between right and wrong?'

The answer is of course that we say what is right, and what is wrong. This is otherwise known as feedback.

In its simplest form it appears as statements such as 'That was good' or 'You shouldn't have done that' or 'That's a bad thing to do'. It is important that we try to match the tone of voice to the nature of the comment, so that the first of those three statements would be said in a warm tone of voice, whereas the last two would be said in a sterner tone.

Some guide-lines for verbal feedback:

The manner in which we give verbal feedback is important. It is meant to be helpful, not 'going on' at the person concerned. Possibly the best image to have is that of a sports coach. Indeed, in some extreme behaviour units the care-staff are actually termed 'coaches'. On the other hand, we don't want to overload the person with good advice, so mainly we are like a friend, but sometimes we are a coach.
Try to make feedback positive. In other words try to notice when clients do things appropriately. In Blanchard's words *'Catch them out doing something right'*.

'Mainly we are like a friend,
but sometimes we are a coach'

Negative verbal feedback should normally be done in private, in brief, and as soon as possible. It is sometimes a mistake to get into discussion - or, more often, an argument - over the feedback.

Positive verbal feedback can be given immediately after the event in question, but can sometimes benefit from being given some time later, for example when reflecting over the day.

When negative feedback is given, it is usually best to say what the client should have done instead of what he or she actually did. Otherwise known as **Constructive Criticism.**

When giving positive feedback it is worth remembering to spot 'Higher Order characteristics such as self control, kindness, persistence, etc.' These are sometimes relatively 'invisible' and we therefore forget to tell the client about them. 'Catch them out doing something right'

It is usually best to match the tone of voice to the nature of the feedback. In other words, positive feedback might be given in a warm tone of voice, whereas negative feedback might be in a sterner tone. I recollect listening to two of my daughter's friends discussing how much they hated a particular teacher. They hated her with such enthusiasm that I couldn't help but enquire what it was about her that made her so awful. They we unequivocal in their reply: 'It's the way she smiles when she tells you off,' they told me. A living example of the importance of 'congruence' – the idea that your tone and manner should match the message.

Tip: Sometimes, feedback is as well given before the next instance, rather than after the last. For example, if someone misbehaves at a group meal they are taken out to, we can do well to give constructive feedback just before going out next time, even if that is a long time later. Why do we give it straight away? Mainly because we don't think we'll remember it for next time. (In which case, how will our client?) The advantage of the 'delayed' system is that the person can immediately improve, rather than feel bad about what they have done.

Tip 2: When giving someone feedback, we do well if we can somehow relate it to the individuals' own future and their goals. After all, people are unlikely to take too much notice of feedback unless it relates to their own aspirations

Tip 3: People take more notice of feedback from someone they judge 'know what they're talking about' than from someone they don't. If you are working as part of a staff group, therefore, feedback is best left to one of the staff member s who is most respected by the specific client. This will vary from client to client.

Feedback also comes in other varieties. Notably: visual feedback and videotaped feedback.

Personally, I wouldn't give much thought to videotaped feedback because it is so easy to use it - wrongly - to 'show up' the person concerned. That is to videotape a sequence of him or her doing whatever dreadful extreme behaviour they do and show it to them to 'teach them a lesson'. My feeling is that that's more likely to be destructive than useful.

It is of course possible to obtain a sequence of the person behaving 'right', for example Ben walking away from Alan when Alan tries to wind him up, but these sequences tend to be very difficult to obtain. Somehow or other they tend not to happen when the videorecorder is running. So, personally, I would resist the temptation that hand-held recorders pose.

Visual feedback - charts etc. - on the other hand I think is excellent and combines very well indeed with verbal feedback, which we discussed earlier.

Visual feedback mainly means charts and drawings, although it might be taken to include tokens that people earn. (Indeed, there is some evidence that the mechanism that is really making 'token economies' work is the feedback they provide, rather than the rewards.)

So let's confine ourselves to charts for the time being. The main factors that make these work, in my experience, are:

- The amount of thought you put into exactly what you are going to measure on a chart. For example if you are working with someone who has a weight problem, would the chart give them feedback about their weight, the quality of their diet, or the degree to which they are exercising?

- The degree to which you make the chart at the right 'level' for the person concerned. That is, a simple, vivid chart for some people, relatively complex and intriguing chart for others.

The intriguing thing about feedback is that it is such an immensely powerful tool and will frequently have a very good effect with people even if it is not attached to any 'reinforcer'. In other words, feedback seems to be reinforcing in its own right.

Incidentally, my own answer to the question above is that I would be inclined to give a person visual feedback on the quality of their diet (i.e. how much and how often they are eating) and, perhaps, how much exercise they are getting. I would be inclined to refrain from giving them feedback on their weight because there is such a big time lag between altering your diet/exercise and seeing any benefit in terms of your weight. Therefore, to make a healthy diet and good exercise *aims in their own right* seems to be the best way forward, allowing the right weight to follow in their wake.

In summary, feedback is an immensely powerful tool that can have profound effects even without any other interventions. Feedback can be verbal, visual, or videotaped. Probably the first two of these are very important and perhaps the last is best avoided. The effectiveness of feedback will depend to a great deal (a) how carefully you choose the information you feed back to the person, and (b) how well your chart or verbal feedback matches up with what the person is prepared to accept.

Exercise:

1. Choose a particular person you are currently working with, to address in this exercise

2. Devise an intervention to help this person, that relies *solely on feedback.* Be very explicit, below, on what you'll be giving feedback about, and exactly how you would give the feedback (verbally, charts, both?)

3. If you are going to use charts, describe exactly the charts you would use, what would be recorded on them, how often they would be filled in, how you would make them interesting for the person concerned, and so on.

Chapter 23:

What to do when Red behaviour happens: Option 4, Addressing the Issue

There are times when we have ignored or played down extreme behaviour and, more to the point, pushed in as much Green behaviour as we know how and yet we still feel that we should do more. Fundamentally we feel we should address the issue. This can sometimes be a good thing because it enables the client and you to discuss what is right and wrong, what is green and red.

So how to discuss the issue constructively and helpfully? Several points:

- *Timing: Choose a time when both the client and you are well disposed to each other! A time you are likely to reach an agreement.*
- *Look to the future, not the past.*
- *Negotiate an agreement. This is usually a compromise, so be prepared for that!*
- *Arrange to discuss again. Very rarely is a problem behaviour sorted out in one discussion.*

In some ways this is similar to contracting, discussing the issue and reaching a clear agreement. In this case however there is no need to have anything written down, although that is an option.

Case Study:

Mary, a 40-year old parent, was concerned about the late time at which her daughter, Norina, came home. Although they had agreed, so Mary thought, that 16-year old Norina should be back home from 'clubbing' by midnight preferably, or by 1am at the latest, this had now drifted so that Norina was routinely back at around 3am on many Friday and Saturday nights.

At first, because the process had been gradual and because she did not want to have a row with Norina, Mary let it go. But finally, after another night spent worrying as to what had happened to her daughter, Mary angrily confronted Norina when she returned home, again at around 3am. Mary's worry came out as anger with her daughter, and in truth there was also an element of anger in it because she felt that her daughter was disobeying her and taking no notice of the agreement they had reached some time previously. Mary insisted on knowing what Norina had been doing until that time of night, and Norina, equally angrily, told her that it was none of her business. The interchange ended when Mary told her daughter that, from now on she would be back by midnight 'whether she liked it or not'. This led, in her mother's words, to Norina 'flouncing off to her room' and both passed a very disturbed night.

Nevertheless, within three days or so, and before another Friday or Saturday, both mother and daughter were getting on well with each other again. Mary seized her opportunity to address the issue. A large part of her was reluctant to do so because she did not want to 'spoil the fact that we were getting on by bringing up something 'difficult'. Nevertheless, she raised the subject by saying to Norina that 'we need to sought out what we're going to do about you going out clubbing ... let's sit down and talk about it properly' and that is what they did.

Mary explained that she was worried about Norina's safety, her reputation, and whether Norina was really doing what she wanted to do. Norina reciprocated by reassuring her mother and trying to explain to her that if she left a club at the kind of time that her mother wanted her to, she would lose credibility in the eyes of her friends.

They reached a compromise where by Norina promised she would phone up her mother some time between midnight and 1am next time, and, in any event, would ensure she was back by 3am. They both felt very pleased with themselves at reaching such an 'adult' compromise, and agreed to discuss things again in two to three weeks.

In summary it is useful to know how to address an issue with someone properly. However it should not be over-used, otherwise you lose the essence of the RAID approach. The main points are:

- *Timing: Choose a time <u>when both the client and you are well disposed to each other</u>! A time you are likely to reach an agreement.*
- *Look to the <u>future</u>, not the past.*
- *Negotiate an agreement. This is usually a compromise, so <u>don't address an issue unless you are prepared to compromise.</u>*
- *Arrange to <u>discuss again</u>. Very rarely is a problem behaviour sorted out in one discussion.*

Chapter 24:

What to do when Red behaviour happens: Option 5, Benign Punishment

I used to call this section simply 'punishment'. Then I had a letter from an irate person who had read the word 'punishment' in the advertising literature for the RAID course. Although she had not attended the course she criticised me roundly for even mentioning such a word in the context of working with people who – often - already have a lot going against them in their lives.

So I have re-named it 'benign punishment' in the hope of clearly getting across the message that, even in this section, we are still working to help the individual. Let me give you a couple of examples:

Example 1 is a guy called Oliver, aged 32. At the age of 24 he had sustained a severe head injury through a road traffic accident. As a result his head, and indeed his brain, were now a different shape. The effect on him had been very interesting inasmuch as his intellectual functioning was remarkably unchanged. He could still talk very sensibly, analyse problems, and hold a thoroughly interesting and entertaining conversation all quite easily. His motor-co-ordination had been effected slightly in that he didn't walk in such a co-ordinated way as he had done previously. But, above all, his inhibitory mechanisms had been impaired.

This meant that he was more inclined to do those things he felt like doing. And one of the most noticeable things he felt like doing was to grab hold of passing females. Sometimes this was a member of staff, sometimes it was another patient. Understandable this had led to him being compulsorily detained ever since he had made a physical recovery from the road traffic accident. Therefore, at the point in time that he came into our treatment unit, he had been compulsorily detained for eight years.

Unfortunately, in spite of a predominantly positive approach he continued to grab hold of passing females just as much as ever he had done. This meant, as it had done for the last eight years, that he was unable to walk around by himself - even in the grounds of the hospital - outside of the locked ward on which he was contained. There was certainly no prospect of him venturing beyond the grounds of the hospital.

The problem with such behaviour as he exhibited is, by definition, that it is intrinsically reinforcing; reinforcing in and of itself. Therefore ignoring it or playing it down is unlikely to get very far and, however much other green behaviour we funnel into him, he will still find it reinforcing to grab hold of passing females. I say 'by definition' because it was his inhibitory centre that was damaged; in other words he was more inclined to do whatever was intrinsically reinforcing to him.

To talk generally for a moment: the concept I have in mind when I use the term 'benign punishment' has several defining characteristics:
- *It is a planned strategy, not simply an immediate response to a problem*
- *It is a treatment strategy, in other words designed to improve the condition of the patient concerned*
- *If successful it will benefit the patient.*

Against this we have the problems associated with punishment, which we described near the beginning of the book. Principally these are ethical (mainly that we cannot do things that society would find unacceptable) and practical (mainly in terms of the 'countercontrol' or 'reactance' that most people display to unwelcome means of controlling their behaviour).

In the RAID Approach we sit down with the patient and obtain their proper, informed, consent to a punishment programme, if that is what we believe to be the best option. But why should anybody agree to being punished, I hear you ask. The answer is just for the reason above, namely that it will benefit them.

So in this particular example I sat down with Oliver and put it to him that 'if only we could retrain his brain to inhibit him from grabbing hold of females' then there would be tremendous benefits for him. Principally that he would (a) be able to walk around the 100 acres of hospital grounds by himself and, eventually, (b) take trips into town and elsewhere by himself.

These were important benefits for him and I suggested that one way that might retrain his brain to achieve this was if the staff would put him in the 'time-out room' for 3 minutes every time he grabbed hold of somebody. He was slightly dubious about this, as probably anybody would be, but on the other hand could see the benefits associated with it. The 'time-out room', by the way, was a room of around 3 metres by 3 metres with no furniture in but an unbreakable glass (actually a plastic) window overlooking the courtyard. The room was painted a light shade of pink and was locked for the 3-minute period.

Eventually, after a few minutes of consideration, he decided to agree to the programme and that he and I would monitor his progress. In fact this was relatively easy to do because it was standard procedure to record any incident when a patient was in the time-out room. Therefore, simply by the time-out room records we had a perfect account of the frequency with which he grabbed hold of somebody.

So that was the programme that was implemented. Gradually, and in a zigzag fashion, the frequency with which he grabbed hold of people declined. After about five months it reached zero and shortly after that he was allowed out into the grounds unaccompanied for short periods. These periods became longer and longer, although he was covertly monitored to ensure the safety of others. Similarly, three months later, he was allowed regular trips into town, and again he was covertly monitored to ensure others' safety.

In summary, my perception is that Oliver benefited greatly from this programme which involved very small degrees of punishment, and I'm not even sure that he found spending three minutes in the time-out room aversive *at all*. Yet the net result was that after having spent eight years compulsorily detained he was, within the space of about eight months, able to go firstly into the hospital grounds and then into town on an unaccompanied basis.

On the down side I feel slightly uneasy that his agreement to the punishment may well have been influenced by his knowledge that if things continued as they were he was likely to be compulsorily detained forever more. On the other hand, that was the reality of the situation, and no doubt a factor that he took into account in a considered way. On balance I am convinced that the programme was immensely to his benefit, the punishment had little or no aversive value to it but was simply punishment in the technical sense, i.e. it reduced the frequency of the behaviour that preceded it. Finally, I am sure that an essential ingredient of that intervention was Oliver's active agreement and participation in the monitoring of progress.

Another example is as follows ...

Penny was a woman of 29 who was diagnosed as suffering from schizophrenia. As a result of her illness she committed various illegal acts, which resulted in her appearing in court and, subsequently, being imprisoned. Whilst in prison she received anti-psychotic medication which largely controlled the main elements of her illness.

One important facet that remained, however, was that she continuously emitted very loud and ear-piercing screams. Not only was this very wearing audibly, but her facial contortions added to the disturbing effect it had on others.

Eventually she was transferred from prison to our treatment unit where the medication was continued, and continued to control most of the symptomatology. Equally the positive, RAIDing-type regime was implemented and we hoped to see a decrease in her screaming. We were disappointed, after three months with us she was screaming just as much as when she first came in.

We spent a lot of time talking about her and producing various theoretical formulations. However, it was not until one of the nursing staff recounted how he had overheard her talking to a fellow patient as they watched, on T.V, a grand procession making its way through London in front of crowds of thousands. 'I'd love to be down there and have a good scream' said Penny to her fellow patient. This gave us the clue that really, to Penny, her screaming was intrinsically reinforcing. So, no matter how pleasurable we made the rest of her life, she would continue to scream so long as she got so much pleasure from it and so little down side to it.

So again, just like with Oliver, we sat down and discussed and agreed benign punishment intervention. Again I used the phraseology of 'retraining the brain' which, although I sometimes think it is a little simplistic, seems to go down well with most people, rather as though it is 'the two of us against the brain'. It seems as though there is some implication that the red behaviour doesn't really belong to the person concerned, but rather belongs to their brain. Therefore Penny and I, or Oliver and I, can work to retrain that bit of brain.

Anyway, we went through the pros and cons of an exactly similar procedure to that we did with Oliver. In other words, the plan was that every time Penny screamed she would be put in the 'time-out room' for three minutes. The pay-off in Penny's case was very similar too. Given that her psychotic symptomatology was very largely controlled apart from the screaming, she would be able to be out and about once that problem was sorted.

Again we had the ready-made measure of progress in the time-out records. In Penny's case, her decline in screaming went very quickly to about 10% of what it had been previously. That took about three to four weeks. Then there was a fairly long tail on the graph where the remaining 10% took two to three months to finally come down to zero.

Just as with Oliver, Penny took to walking around the grounds, taking trips into town and, most rewardingly, applied for and obtained a job as a secretary that was advertised in the local newspaper, and that she obtained against open competition.

It is possible to feel the same mixed feelings as before, but to me it felt overwhelmingly that Penny had agreed to a programme that benefited her immensely in exchange for little or no cost. Having seen the video tape of her screaming in prison and comparing that now with the young woman who was commuting to her job in town there was little short of a transformation. I don't think she had found her spells in the time-out room punishing in any real sense although technically they were a punishment in that they reduced the frequency of the screaming behaviour. And again I'm sure it was very important that she gave her real, considered agreement to the programme and that we constantly monitored her progress together.

So I hope those two examples get across what I mean as benign punishment. <u>Some small or negligible cost that nevertheless eradicates the behaviour in question</u>. It is important that the person properly agrees to it and that he or she has full involvement throughout, particularly in terms of monitoring the progress. Just as important is that the RAID philosophy that we have been talking about throughout remains in place. That the benign punishment for a particular specified behaviour is against the background of a system of relationships, philosophy and interventions that is overwhelmingly positive. In

terms of our pictorial model I - perhaps rather strangely - imagine it that not only are we pouring in nice green fluid into the funnel but we are also gently sucking out the red from the far end of the syringe.

Chapter 25:

What to do when Red behaviour happens:

Option 6, Sanctions

It could be argued that talk of sanctions does not really belong in this manual but, nevertheless, conversation I've had with professionals over the years suggests to me that it is worth including a few words.

By sanctions what I mean is 'consequences for an action which are not necessarily designed to help or improve the individual but are imposed primarily to act as a deterrent to others'.

I'd suggest that there are several points that need to be made about sanctions:

1. The individual has to be compus mentis before sanctions are ethical. In other words if a window is broken by someone who knew what he was doing then you might (or might not) choose to impose the sanction of a fine (which would go towards repairing the window). However if the same window was broken by somebody during a psychotic episode it would probably be seen by most people as unethical to impose any sanctions.
2. I have come across people who - even in secure facilities for very disturbed behaviour - say that sanctions should be employed because 'that's what happens outside'. Personally I disagree with the idea that 'that's what happens outside' is any sort of reason for applying them 'inside'. The whole reason that patients are in such treatment units is that they cannot adapt to the normal outside environment. Therefore to re-create such an environment seems to me to be folly.
3. In terms of how to 'choose' the sanction (if you have decided that one is definitely necessary) I suggest there are four criteria summarised by the letters R.I.P., standing for:

Relevant, **I**mmediate, **P**roportionate

In other words the sanction should be relevant to whatever it refers to. So, for example, if it is going to cost money to replace a broken pane of glass then perhaps a fine would be a relevant sanction. Incidentally, the fine does not have to be the same value as the cost of replacing the pain; it can simply be put *towards* the cost of replacing the glass.

It should be immediate, simply to make a psychological link between the action that is taken and the consequence. Although we said earlier that sanctions are implemented 'to encourage the others - regardless of whether it helps the individual or not' it is nevertheless sensible to maximise the chances of it improving the individual's behaviour.

Proportionate is a very difficult concept because what's proportionate to one person is disproportionate to another. Nevertheless, it is a key concept. The yardstick I use is whether 12 good people – e.g. a jury - would see the sanction as proportionate if I had to stand up and describe it in a court of law. One other point here is that sometimes a professional will ask the client to put forward what sanction they think is right, and I'm convinced this is a major mistake. Sometimes clients are much too hard on themselves and, from the professional's point of view, one cannot begin to justify the imposition of a specific sanction on the basis that 'the client suggested it'.

I mentioned earlier that there were four criteria summarised by the three letters. The fourth criterion is to 'let it rest'. In other words if you feel the necessity to impose a sanction then, once it has been imposed, that should be the end of the matter. Hence the 'Rest In Peace' message of the acronym.

Chapter 26:

A Yardstick For Judging How We Responded

So there are a lot of techniques which we can use in a heated situation. But in truth we end up simply doing what we can. In those situations it is helpful to have a yardstick for judging what we have done or, better still, what we are about to do.

There are 3 principal considerations:

- **Whatever we do must, of course, be *ethical*.**

- **We try hard not to do anything that might damage the *relationship* between the client and ourselves.**

- **Even in our intervention we try to *set a good example*.**

Section Four: In conclusion

Chapter 27:

Coping With Our Own Feelings

It is easy to talk of the counsel of perfection, as though extreme behaviour does not affect us emotionally. That would be false, most people who work with extreme behaviour are significantly affected by it. Sometimes that emotional effect means that we do not act as we would wish to. For this reason it is important to look at how we can cope with our own feelings.

I confess to being short of terrific ideas in this area, but here are one or two:

- *Remember that we operate our own standards. So although our client may sulk or may even hit us, we do not do either of these; we have our own rules for ourselves.*

- *There are times when we simply need a few minutes 'time out' to calm down and get a grip again. Take it if you can.*

- *Talking to friends and colleagues takes a lot of beating. Not just immediately after a taxing incident, but later too, to wind down.*

- *Looking after ourselves in simple things like getting enough sleep, exercise, nutrition, and not too much alcohol, caffeine and nicotine can help.*

- *Act as your own best friend. When really agitated or worn down ask yourself 'If I had the best friend in the world, someone who was all-wise and only had my interests at heart, what would they tell me to do, right now.'*

You have probably found some good ideas of your own. If you can think of any now, do write them in below to develop a checklist.

Chapter 28:

Higher Order RAIDing

Rationale

So far we have spoken about reinforcing specific behaviours that people do. We have emphasised the importance of spotting the good behaviours and, in particular, spotting progress. We have spoken about how important it is to be able to reinforce such behaviour effectively. How, sometimes, what a person finds reinforcing is very small - very subtle - indeed. Furthermore, a client can find it condescending for a member of staff to praise him in an over-the-top fashion.

We can go a step further. It is possible to reinforce not just particular behaviours, but also personality characteristics.

Once we develop the ability to do this we really have the power to increase the person's self-image, their sense of self-efficacy and their self-esteem. We are now not just increasing the likelihood of adaptive behaviours and decreasing the frequency of extreme ones, we are really getting to the core of the person.

So what sort of traits and characteristics might we be looking at ....

◊ Being empathic
◊ Having self-control
◊ Being assertive
◊ Being careful
◊ Being friendly
◊ Being determined/persistent
◊ Being self-sufficient
◊ Being honest
◊ Having pride
◊ Being caring
◊ Being 'fun'

Again, which, if any of these will be best for a specific individual, is part of one's clinical judgement. But what if we set ourselves a difficult general question such as: What characteristics should we reinforce? What answers might we come up with? Some possibilities might be:

Answer 1: 'Adaptive' characteristic that the person possesses anyway. These may not be characteristics that you personally value, or that seem directly important in the individual's development. Nevertheless, noticing and commenting on them boosts the self-image and self-esteem of the person concerned.

Answer 2: Particular characteristics that are relevant to 'target'. These are characteristic(s), highly relevant to the client's progress. So, for example, 'self-control' might very well be one. If so, we would be vigilant in spotting instances of the client displaying self-control, and reinforce it.

Possibly the best example of how these two answers fit together is in working with children. Or indeed in bringing up one's own children. In these cases you start by valuing the characteristics that the youngster naturally possesses (answer 1, above), but you may seek to develop other characteristics which you believe will be to the youngster's advantage - honesty, for example - but which they may have in only a small measure (answer 2 above),

So how do we reinforce such characteristics ....

Answer 1: By feedback. In other words you tell the person as soon as possible:
'that was good self control" or
'you're getting properly assertive' or
'you're developing a lot of determination'
or whatever the characteristic is.

Two points.

First, the person concerned may never have come across the phrase 'self-control' or 'assertiveness' or whatever characteristic you are referring to. The first time you use it he or she may wonder what you are talking about. This does not matter. With repeated use most people will eventually pick it up, even if it is phrase that is not very often used in the wider world. So they will eventually conceptualise themselves as 'someone with self control'. The pay-off for this, for both you and your client, is that at crucial moments you will eventually be able to prompt him or her: *'Use your self-control.'*

The second point is that this feedback can be delayed. So you might, for example, say: *'I thought you showed some good self-control this morning, when Alan was trying to wind you up.'* The best tone of voice is normally a matter of fact one, in these circumstances; the danger is that, otherwise, you may come over as condescending.

Answer 2: By feedback and guided discovery. In other words you say something like: *'I thought that was great self-control this morning, when Alan was trying to wind you up and you didn't respond. How did you manage that?'* Again, in a matter of fact tone. The reply might be: *'Well I just walked away from it.'* Which you might decide is enough, or you might continue with, *'Does that normally work well?'* Which might elicit the response: *'It does if I can't think of anything to say.'* At which stage you might decide to finish the conversation with: *'Well it certainly worked well this morning.'*

Note: Guided discovery is a technique often used in Cognitive Therapy, and its use in the example above is twofold:

θ   First it makes clearer a rule that may not yet have been in the client's mind. Namely, in this case: *'If someone is winding you up and you can't think of what to say back, the best thing to do is to walk away.'*
θ   Second, it empowers' the client. He or she gradually realises that they possess a good deal of expertise themselves, and can - to some extent - sort out their own problems.

Pushing at the Boundaries

"When we treat a man as he is, we make him worse than he is. When we treat him as if he already is what he could be, we make him what he should be." Goethe.

There is an old English folk story about two brothers who were caught stealing sheep near their village. In complete fury, the local villagers hauled both brothers down to the local blacksmith and had each branded 'ST' on their forehead, so everyone would know they were Sheep Thieves.

Both brothers were very ashamed. One went out of the cottage only rarely, and would get a lot of food in so that he could stay there as long as possible, he couldn't bear the shame. The other was equally ashamed, and so resolved to travel to a distant part of the country and keep himself to himself there.

When he arrived in his new village he left his lodgings only occasionally, but nevertheless became the talk of the village-folk, all wondering why he should have the letters 'ST' on his forehead. Discussion went to and fro over weeks and months until finally a consensus was reached. His humble demeanour and manner of keeping himself apart decided them that he must be a SainT.

From then on the villagers treated the brother with great respect, and he, not realising what had happened gradually responded. They looked to him for advice about troubles that beset them and for help when that was needed. He willingly obliged, happy to be treated that way and eager to redeem himself for his previous misdeeds. In that way he lived out his remaining years happily and profitably for all around.

Empathy: A Special Note

Empathy certainly deserves special treatment. It cannot simply be lumped in together with all the other personal characteristics, even at the top of the list. It is not only the characteristic which marks out the best therapists, it is also the one which underpins much socialised and 'Appropriate' behaviour.

It has not always been a concept which has found much favour. Thomas Hobbes, in his Leviathan (1651) felt that in a state of nature people would either kill each other immediately or quietly 'dread and distrust each other'. Perhaps this is to be expected from someone who witnessed the Civil War at first hand and is reputed to have a severed head once land in his lap, but he was not alone in his view. Baruch Spinoza, Dutch lens grinder and unreadable philosopher, maintained that people think only of themselves: 'In their desires and judgements of what is beneficial, people are always carried away by their passions which take no account of the future or anyone else.'

It was left to Scotsman David Hume in his Enquiry Concerning the Principles of Morals (1751) to recognise that many of our passions are based on what he called sympathy, by which he meant the capacity to experience powerfully in oneself the sufferings and joys of others.

So if we can help people to develop empathy they may be as motivated to reduce the suffering of others almost as much as if it were their own. So how can we do this? Predominantly by two ways:

1) Asking *'how would you like it if ...'* questions, as in *'How would you like it if someone twice your size came up to you and took whatever he wanted of yours, and hit you if you didn't give it to him?'* Note: it is important to ask in a tone of voice which allows the listener to imagine it, rather than in a punitive tone which prevents that; the idea in this instance is to develop empathy .

2) Drawing a parallel in the life of the listener. For example, where someone says *'Why is Tony so upset, just because he's not allowed to go and see Star Wars on Saturday ... I don't even like Star Wars',* the reply can be along the lines *of 'Yes but remember Tony really likes Star Wars ... it's like Man United were playing here on Saturday, you had a ticket and were all set to go to the match with your best mates, and then someone said they weren't going to allow you to go'* (where the listener is an ardent Man United fan).

Note: Paradoxically, it can be difficult for empathic people to realise that some people have little empathy, and therefore need such situations as the above explained to them. Nevertheless, some do, and, done repeatedly, it is one good way of developing empathy.

Chapter 29:

Traps For RAIDers

1. **Only half of the acronym is remembered:** either the RA half or the ID half, but not both. So, for example, the staff member reinforces appropriate behaviour but also responds to difficult and disruptive behaviour. Or, conversely, the difficult behaviour is ignored, but so is appropriate behaviour. If you are going to remember only one half, make it **RA.** If your clients are busy behaving appropriately all the time, they will have no time left for extreme behaviour!

2. **Always a Step Behind.** This is a common temptation: it is where the person comes out with difficult or disruptive behaviour, and we manage to 'let it go' - to Ignore it in other words. Then, shortly afterwards, s/he is behaving impeccably. What should we do? We know what we *should* do, we should switch to reinforcing such behaviour. Just gently and naturally, just responding in an ordinary way. But what do we do? A little voice inside us somewhere says *'I'm blowed if s/he is going to get round me that easily. 5 minutes ago s/he was behaving like a *** and now they think they can just forget all about it.'* And so on! So now we are the one who is sulking. Or even, sometimes, we take advantage of the restored communication to have a go at the person about how badly s/he behaved 5 minutes ago. Leaving them thinking *'Well if this is what I get for behaving better, I'm not going to bother'* or words to that effect.

3. **Reinforcing is done 'Over The Top'.** Remember Aristotle's Golden Mean. Over-the-top reinforcement can be counterproductive, because the recipient perceives it as being either manipulative or condescending. In either case the individual is unlikely to respond as one would hope, and one can even generate *counter-control,* where the client, apparently deliberately, behaves in the reverse direction from what you hope for.

4. **Life is *too* secure.** This is one of the *less* likely traps to fall into, but nevertheless deserves a mention. Bowlby discusses 'the secure base, within and from which one explores the world', and this is a graphic way of envisaging what we provide for our clients. However, it is possible that we make the client's base so secure that s/he receives a tremendous shock when going into the real world: people are much less positive and much more critical than they have become accustomed to. The danger of that is that s/he then 'writes off' the feedback that we have been giving as 'false', and understandably takes little notice of anything subsequent that we say. The answer is that the secure base is in terms of *unconditional positive regard,* but we also give a

degree of accurate feedback, concentrating mainly - but not exclusively - on *positive* aspects. RAIDing, in other words.

The reason that this is one of the less likely traps to fall into is that - on account of our 'human-ness' - we tend to give some feedback on negative aspects of a client's behaviour, even though we are trying 100% to adopt a RAID approach.

5. **Ignoring is used as a weapon**. This usually leads to counter-control (see later) where the person thinks of something even more extreme s/he can do, and effectively challenges you to ignore that!
Note: If we are Ignoring correctly it is impossible to use it as a weapon, because 'correct' ignoring means 'not focusing on the extreme behaviour'. Incorrect ignoring, the type that can be used as a weapon, involves ignoring the person, as in giving them 'the silent treatment', which has nothing at all to do with the RAID approach.

6. **Counter-control**. Counter-control is the term given to what is colloquially referred to as bloody-mindedness. The phenomenon whereby people sometimes seem to deliberately push against us.

One of the main causes of this is the use of punishment. Almost as though the person receiving the punishment says to him or herself *'If you think you can control me that way, I'll show you how wrong you are.'*

But Counter-control *can* also take place when positive methods are used. What is intended as social reinforcement - phrases such as 'well done' and so forth - can actually be interpreted as condescending or manipulative and therefore have the opposite effect.

Similarly token or points programmes can be seen in that light - condescending or manipulative. Likewise, other programmes which result in even positive consequences for specified behaviours. They can all result in that same response from the recipient: *'If you think you are going to control my behaviour that way, I'll show you how wrong you are.'*

However, there are some clear cut solutions ...

AVOIDING COUNTERCONTROL AND REACTANCE

1. *Avoid the use of punishment an sanctions as far as possible.* Punishment from us often results in punishment from the recipient and the danger of an escalating conflict situation. Hence the RAID® approach.

2. *Ensure that the social reinforcement is neither condescending nor manipulative.* In other words that it is genuine and pays proper respect to the client.

3. *Obtain the client's co-operation in designing their own plans-for-change.* Clients rarely go against programmes they have been involved in designing. This can even, or perhaps especially, be the case in designing token / points programmes; some clients have a very good sense of what should be required to earn specific rewards.

4. *It is sometimes a good idea not to specify that you are reinforcing appropriate behaviour and ignoring difficult behaviour.* Again, this invites the client to see it as manipulation, even though the intention is to be in the client's best interests. It is usually best for matters to appear almost accidental: when the client behaves green things somehow go well, when he or she behaves in a red way their behaviour is ignored, or at least played down.

Note: Although it is probably a bad idea to specify that you are reinforcing green behaviour and ignoring red behaviour, there is no harm at all in describing the RAID philosophy in general terms. A phrase such as *'What we do here is to play to everyone's strengths and develop them, and play down the problem side of things'* describes it well.

Chapter 30:

Deeply RAIDing

The essence of Deeply RAIDing is to move from using RAID as a technique to really believing in what you are doing.

Some people find this really easy; they believe in it straight away, others find it a little more difficult. One of the frequent problems is in *truly* Ignoring Difficult or Disruptive behaviour. Not just doing it as a technique, but really not letting it get to you.

On the following pages, and in the course content and exercises, you might find some encouragement in doing just that. I hope so, because to really Ignore Difficult and Disruptive, rather than pretending to, can make all the difference; not just for your clients, but for you too.

Some Common Problems

One of the problems that some people have when they come to adopt the RAID approach is that, although they recognise intellectually that it is just what they should be doing, they are hampered by unspoken beliefs they harbour somewhere inside themselves. Beliefs such as:

'I must always be in total control of everything clients do.'

'I must point out to people every mistake they make.'

'People must not do things which I wouldn't do, or which irritate me.'

'I can - or should be able to - influence every last aspect of a client/employee. '

If any of these look rather familiar to you, or you own up to something a bit different but similar, there are two simple things you can do:

1) Think of an alternative sentence that contradicts the one above, and adopt it as yours', and

2) Change what you do to fit in with your new sentence. Your new behaviour will help you *truly* believe your new belief.

Looking After the RAIDers

Working with people who display extreme behaviour is demanding work. It is bound to be; by definition it is.

This means that we have to be reasonably conscientious in looking after ourselves. It is much more difficult to keep our focus on positive, constructive behaviour from clients when we ourselves are feeling below par. So what are the main areas to focus on? No doubt you know yourself better than anyone else does, you know what things you have to attend to, in order to keep up to scratch, but in general there are five main areas for attention:

Biological factors, such as: Sleep, Nutrition, Exercise, Moderation in alcohol, caffeine, other drugs, Pain, Control of undue tension, by relaxation.

Environmental factors (including the social environment). Any environmental factors either at home or at work, which cry out for change in some way?

Social factors. For example: Have you got at least one or two people at work with whom you can talk uninhibitedly about significant matters that crop up? Although we try to keep 'our private life' quite separate from work, are there issues there that need addressing? It is easy for these to spill over into work, even with the best of intentions on our part. Do we maintain a social life quite apart from work and our domestic / intimate relationships? For many - but not all - people, it is important to do so.

Behavioural factors: Are we aiming for achievable goals? If we simply ask too much of ourselves - either over-scheduling or trying to attain the impossible - no technique can rescue us. Are we scheduling in things that are purely for enjoyment? Some people are good at doing this in leisure time but not at work; some in the reverse. Ideally we have occasional 'pure pleasure items' at work and in leisure.

Cognitive factors: Do we give ourselves an unduly hard time through our **'automatic thoughts'?** Things like Jumping to (negative) conclusions, Focussing on the negative side of things and down-playing the positive, Over-generalising from one thing that goes wrong, or Putting it down to yourself when something bad happens at work?

So all of these are probably things we know already, and in any event it is pretty tough trying to keep track of all of them all of the time. Even so, the better job we do on these, the easier it is to focus on the positive as far as our clients are concerned. As ever, it means it is good for us and good for our clients too.

RAID® Review

In an area of few happy coincidences it is good to note that the RAID approach exemplifies one. Although the approach - always emphasising positive aspects and playing down negative ones - evolved purely as the most *effective* one, it is fortuitous that it helps us to keep up our own motivation much more actively than does a *problem-focused* way of working.

When we know that the effectiveness of any technique is underpinned by a strong relationship between helper and helped, and a positive, optimistic, energetic and collaborative attitude from the helper, it is as well that the RAID approach meshes perfectly with such attitudes. To a degree, it actually engenders them.

But this is not to say that now, at last, working with people who display extreme behaviours is unrelenting fun. It can be fun, it can be rewarding, possibly more so than many other areas of work. But it is also demanding, and it can be very frustrating. At times we feel that nothing we do is helping particular clients, and that is demoralising.

It is at times like that we fall back on the knowledge that what we are doing is not only the way most likely to succeed, it is also the right way. It keeps up our relationship with the clients and sets a good example for them to follow.

Even so, there will be times when we feel we have 'let ourselves down'. We have 'lost our cool' or whatever way we like to phrase it. But maybe this is not too bad a thing. It is perhaps as well that our clients know that we are human! And perhaps it is also as well that they have just a little preparation for the frustration that one person can cause in another.

But often we look back over a heated incident, and we ask ourselves *'did I do right?'* Were we right to remain controlled in the face of extreme provocation, or does that somehow seem 'un-natural' or 'inhuman'? I would suggest that the RAID acronym cuts through a lot of that, but that there are also two questions we can ask ourselves, if we really want an answer to the question *'Was I right?'* These are:

What effect will our reaction have had on our relationship with the person concerned? And

What sort of an example have we set?

Thank you for reading this book. I hope that you find the RAID® approach an effective and enjoyable way of working.

**William Davies,
Thurnby, 2000**

Chapter 31:

RAID® References

These references are written in a non-conventional style, so that you can tell what each reference contains, without referring back to the text.

The D.R.O. (differential reinforcement of other behaviour) and D.R.I. (differential reinforcement of incompatible behaviour) methods are described in most behavioural texts. That in *Behaviour Modification in the Human Services* is probably as good as any. Authors: Sundel, S.S. and Sundel, M. Published in 1993 by Sage, Newbury Park, California. They also cite some references as to its efficacy.

Probably the best description of how important cognitive factors (predominantly our thoughts) are in behavioural programmes is in M.J.Mahoney's *Cognition and Behaviour Modification*, published by in 1974 by Ballinger, Cambridge, Mass.

Just the right amount of attention is reinforcing, too much can be punishing (study of teachers and pupils)
Epling, W. and Pierce, W. (1988) Applied behaviour analysis: new directions from the laboratory. In G. Davey and C. Cullen (eds) *Human Operant Conditioning and Behaviour Modification.* Wiley, Chichester.

People need to see the rewards they receive as being consequent upon their actions, and if people find that whatever they do they cannot affect the consequences that befall them, then they may become depressed, or the victims of 'learned helplessness'
Seligman, M. (1975) *Helplessness.* W.H.Freeman, San Francisco.

Behaviours closely followed by rewarding consequences are strengthened and more likely to recur in the future under similar circumstances (Thorndike's Law of Effect)
Thorndike, E. (1911) *Animal Intelligence.* Macmillan, New York.

A similar assertion, though preferring the term reinforcement to reward, and suggesting an alternative theory about the underlying processes, is made by Skinner, B.F. (1938) *The Behaviour of Organisms.* Appleton-Century-Crofts, New York.

Activities of low probability can be increased in frequency if activities of high probability are made contingent upon them. (eg 'If you do your homework you can watch the TV.') Known as the Premack Principle.

Premack, D. (1965) Reinforcement theory. In D. Levine (ed.) *Nebraska Symposium on Motivation, Vol. 13,* University of Nebraska Press, Lincoln.

The right amount of reward seems to be more effective than simply very large rewards.
Lawler, E. (1983) Reward systems in organizations. In J. Lorsch (ed.) *Handbook of Organisational Behaviour.* Prentice-Hall, Englewood Cliffs, N.J.

What is rewarding in one situation may not be in another. Eg, attention from a teacher in a classroom may be highly desirable, whereas attention from the same teacher in the playground may be unwelcome.
Epling, W. and Pierce, W. (1988) Applied behaviour analysis: new directions from the laboratory. In G.Davey and C.Cullen (eds) *Human Operant Conditioning and Behaviour Modification.* Wiley, Chichester.

For the role of shaping in acquiring everyday skills such as swimming, driving etc Schwartz, B. (1989) *Psychology of Learning and Behaviour,* Norton, New York.

Skinner maintained that a reinforcer needs simply to follow an action for it to be reinforced, without the organism necessarily being aware of the connection
Skinner, B.F. (1977) The force of coincidence. In B.Etzel, J. Le Blanc and D. Baer (eds) *New Developments in Behavioral Research: Theory, Method and Application.* Lawrence Erlbaum Associates, Hillsdale, N.J.

Whereas Bandura maintains that rewards work best when the individuals involved are aware of the causal relationship between what they have done and the outcome.
Bandura, A. (1986) *Social Learning Theory.* Prentice-Hall, Englewood Cliffs, N.J.

Mahoney points out a major problem that can occur when people are aware of the rules (or 'contingencies') you have set up, namely that of countercontrol. In other words, people may deliberately go against your influences on them, maybe because they see themselves as being manipulated, coerced, condescended to, or whatever. This is especially important if ever one thinks in terms of punishment.
Mahoney, M.J. (1974) *Cognition and Behaviour Modification.* Ballinger, Cambridge, Massachusets

This fighting against the contingencies, especially if those contingencies are predominantly punishments, is graphically described by Boyle, in his account of his life, and, in particular, his prison life.
Boyle, J. (1975) *A Sense of Freedom.*

A phenomenon identical to Mahoney's countercontrol is termed 'reactance' by Brehm and Brehm.

Brehm, S. and Brehm, J. (1981) *Psychological Reactance: A Theory of Freedom and Control.* Academic Press, New York.

People who were committed to giving blood were less likely to give blood when they were offered payment. Upton, W. (1973) Altruism, attribution and intrinsic motivation in the recruitment of blood donors. *Dissertation Abstracts International,* 34, 6260B

It has been suggested that people have an in-built need to deal effectively with the environment. White, R. (1959) Motivation reconsidered: the concept of competence. *Psychological Review,* 66, 297-333.

Bandura in *Social Foundations of Thought and Action: A Social Cognitive Theory.* Prentice Halle, Englewood-Cliffs, N.J. (1986) says that vicarious learning takes place in groups. 'If a person experiences consequences in a group setting, the observed outcomes can affect the behaviour of the group as a whole. Even mild praise or reprimand can lead other group members to adopt praiseworthy acts and to avoid censurable ones.'

Bandura is also foremost amongst those who point to the importance of 'modelling' ... the example we (and others) set.

Turney et al. (1983) highlight the difficulty of a teacher in a large classroom providing individual reinforcement. Under these circumstances, vicarious reinforcement can be put to good use. Turney, C., Eltis, K., Hatton, N., Owen, L., Towler, J. and Wright, R. (1983) *Sydney Micro Skills Redeveloped: Series 1 Handbook.* Sydney University Press, Sydney.

Prue and Fairbank say 'praise publicly - punish privately' Prue, D. and Fairbank, J. (1981) Performance feedback in organizational behaviour management: A review. *Journal of Organizational Behaviour Management,* 3, 1-16.

But public praise can cause embarrassment and therefore be counterproductive {Giacolone, R. and Rosenfeld, P. (1987). Impression management concerns and reinforcement interventions. *Group and Organization Studies,* 12, 445-453.} And people may feel it is unfair, if they have done equally well but receive no praise. Bandura refers to this as the implicit effects of observed consequences; Bandura 86 (see above).

Expectations of self-efficacy are important for a person to carry out any task, even if they anticipate reward. Mischel, W. (1973) Toward a cognitive social learning reconceptualization of personality. *Psychological Review,* 80, 252-283.

A history of past success is one of the most significant determinants of a belief of one's ability to pursue a course of action, Bandura, A., (1989) Self regulation of motivation and action through internal standards and goal;

systems. In L. Pervin (ed.) *Goal Concepts in Personality and Social Psychology.* Lawrence Erlbaum Assocs, Hillsdale, N.J.

Also, the encouragement and support of others can be very important: Baron, R. (1988) Negative effects of destructive criticism: Impact on conflict, self-efficacy, and task performance. *Journal of Applied Psychology*, 73, 199-207.

It is John Bowlby who talks of 'a secure base' which a (helping) relationship can provide, from which to explore the world. This is in, unexpectedly enough, *A Secure Base*, published in 1988 by Basic Books, New York.

Excessively negative and punishing parental practices may be associated with depression, anxiety and low self-esteem in later life. Bryan, J. and Freed, F. (1982) Corporal Punishment: Normative data and sociological and psychological correlates in a community college population. *Journal of Youth and Adolescence*, 11, 77-87.

A rewarding upbringing, especially the mother using verbal rewards, may lead to a positive outlook on life when adult. Gussman, K. and Harder, D. (1990) Offspring Personality and Deceptions of Parental Use of Reward and Punishment. *Psychological Reports*, 67, 923- 930.

As an infant matures it develops a recognition hunger, ie a need to be acknowledged by others as a person in one's own right. Berne, E. (1964) *Games People Play*. Grove Press, New York.

Eric Berne's Transactional Analysis has the concept of strokes. These are interactions between people and can be positive or negative. Stewart (below) maintains that 'any stroke is better than no stroke'. In other words, people would prefer negative strokes such as ridicule, threats and blame to being ignored. Stewart, I. (1989) *Transactional Analysis Counselling in Action*, Sage, London.

William James thought much along the same lines. 'No more fiendish punishment could be devised were such a thing possible, than that one should be turned loose in society and remain absolutely unnoticed by all the members thereof'. James, W. (1890) *The Principles of Psychology*. Holt, New York.

Hence, we have the position, taking the transactional analysis viewpoint, that, if we do not provide attention, notice and rewards for children because of their good behaviour then they will work to obtain such attention (in the form of punishments and blame) by behaving badly. We then have the paradox that our 'punishment' actually reinforces the bad behaviour. (Stewart, 1989, above).

John Bowlby uses the term 'care eliciting' behaviour to describe actions which, unsurprisingly, are designed to elicit care from others. It is a good phrase because of its implication that we should respond to such actions. (Compare with 'attention seeking' which has [wrongly] come to imply that we should ignore 'attention-seeking behaviour'.) Bowlby, J. 1969. *Attachment and Loss, Volume 1: Attachment.* London: Hogarth Press.

Egan refers to Goleman's finding that the relationship between helper and helped is one of the best predictors of the success or otherwise of an intervention. Egan, G. (1990). The Skilled Helper (Fourth Edition). Brooks/Cole, Pacific Grove, California.

Lambert's excellent review demonstrates that it is the helper's 'personal characteristics' more than their 'techniques' which mostly help others improve. Lambert, M.J., Clinical Psychology Review, Vol 9, pp. 469-485, (1989), *'The Individual Therapist's Contribution to Psychotherapy Process and Outcome'.*

British Philosopher Thomas Hobbes (1588-1679) author of *Leviathan* (1651) and Dutch lens grinder philosopher Baruch Spinoza (1632-77) were two of many who held a gloomy view of human nature, believing us to be almost totally self-centred. Charles Darwin (1809-82) added some biological utility to such self-centredness. It's not in Smiths, but Spinoza wrote *Tractatus Theologico-Politicus* (1670).

In *Enquiry Concerning the Principles of Morals* (conveniently published exactly 100 years after Leviathan, ie in 1751) David Hume (1711-76) Scottish author of *History of England,* argued the case of altruism, against such psychological egoism described above. He argued for 'sympathy' by which we can powerfully experience the suffering and joys of others. But a hard-line egoist could still argue that we only help others because it makes us feel good.

Hall and Barker found that the key element of token economies is actually the giving of feedback. Hall, J.N. and Barker, R.D. (1986). Token economies and schizophrenia: a review. In *Contemporay issues in schizophrenia,* (ed. A. Kerr, and R.P. Snaith), pp. 410-19. Gaskell, London.

Faber, A. and Mazlish, E. (1998) in *How to Talk So Kids Will Listen and Listen So Kids Will Talk,* published by Simon and Schustler, are excellent at describing how to give positive feedback to kids in a non-patronising way. Seems good for adults too. The same authors in 1999 wrote the follow-up, *Siblings Without Rivalry,* published by Piccadilly Press, London. A self-help book for parents, this tackles the eponymous age-old problem. Again, some of the concepts from this very readable book apply across the board.

Chapter 32:

A Manager's Checklist:
Is Our Service A RAIDing One?

If you are a manager of a service for people who display extreme behaviour, you might like to check out how your service matches up. Below is a series of statements which we call 'dream statements'. They describe perfection. Underneath each there is a space for you to give your service a rating out of 100, the more the better.

DREAM STATEMENTS:

We operate a clear philosophy of care, known as RAIDing. It means we see the best in people ... we notice predominantly the *good* behaviour that clients emit, and acknowledge or recognise it just right. As this implies, we ignore, or at least play down, the difficult or disruptive behaviour.

Rating: ....

We know that the essence of RAIDing is to push green behaviour into the person. So if we see that someone reacts in a way that is bad for them when they are for example being wound up or being frustrated by something, we do our best to teach them a better way of responding.

Rating: ....

We also RAID in the sense of pushing as much reinforcement into the person's life as we can do. We know that the more reinforcing the person's life is, the less the extreme behaviour will ensue.

Rating: ....

We always recollect why the RAID approach works (building the client, maintaining a good relationship, providing a good model, and providing an appropriate means for our clients to obtain positive attention). This means we can apply it even in new situations.

Rating: ………..

We display the 'Appropriate' personality characteristics. Especially, staff are empathic, constantly positive, energetic, patient, determined, and team players. And we monitor our maintenance of these qualities!

Rating: ………..

Our service provides each person with the right level of relationship from which they can benefit, and we understand that without this relationship we are hardly 'in the game'.

Rating: ………..

We are excellent at ensuring that clients know exactly what is expected of them. We make sure people have a vivid picture of what they are meant to do, right from waking in the morning until going to bed at night. This includes how they are meant to spend their time, what they are to do if they have problems or worries, and how they can best pursue treatment goals. This way, our clients feel secure and that they have a mastery over their time and their life. What is more, all staff are genuinely agreed on what is expected, so we are all pulling in the same direction.

Rating: ………..

In groups of two or more clients, we spot particularly those who are behaving *right,* and gently ensure that they are acknowledged. We are aware of the danger of winding up anyone who is behaving badly by doing this, but we do it subtly enough to avoid that danger!

Rating: ………..

We are terrific at giving feedback in a straightforward, constructive, friendly way. We realise that the point is mainly for the person to know when they are doing *right,* so they can do it again! We are also careful not to overdo it; we know people can have too much feedback, even if it's positive!

Rating: ………..

Staff are excellent at using positive words to describe aspects of clients' personality, to build their self-image and self-esteem.

Rating: ………..

We never tell people what not to do! Rather, we suggest - as gently and as tactfully as we can - what they *should* do, and if we can't think what they should do, we just keep quiet!

Rating: ………..

We avoid asking the obvious *'what shall we do when he comes out of his room in the middle of the night and smashes the place up?'* question, and instead ask a question of the *'how can we get him to sleep through the night?'* type.

Rating: ………..

We are excellent at instilling a sense of the *future* in clients so they have a clear direction and know they are working towards what they want. We are also strong at encouraging and supporting them in achieving those goals.

Rating: ………..

There are some staff who are well able to use the RAID® 4-box functional analysis of extreme behaviour when necessary. Forms are completed objectively and thoroughly, and analysed later to properly determine what underlies the behaviour. A suitable intervention is then chosen. Very often that means simply spotting - and acknowledging - the person doing *especially* well, ie not coming out with extreme behaviour when, from our analysis, we would have been expected to.

Rating: ………..

When we can see the extreme behaviour serves a clear function for the person, we are ingenious at devising a more beneficial way that he or she can achieve that function. This is so even when the function is to obtain attention! We understand that all of us need attention, and it's just a matter of how we go about getting it! And anyway, we know that extreme behaviour can serve all sorts of functions; we are shrewd at working out what they might be, and helping the people achieve them in ways that are better for them.

Rating: ………..

We are good at working out what triggers the extreme behaviour, if anything (and we know there often is). When we have worked it out we know to either:
• get rid of the trigger, or
• teach them to cope with the trigger, or
• reinforce the client when the trigger occurs and s/he doesn't respond badly.

Rating: ………..

We are first rate at judging if an issue needs addressing. If so we choose a good time to address it and do so constructively. In particular we choose a time when the client and we are likely to discuss things rationally with each other, we keep the conversation focused on future solutions rather than past problems, we ensure that we reach some kind of agreement, and we arrange to review progress later on.

Rating: ………..

Our staff know how to handle their feelings when extreme behaviour does occur. Although we know that we will probably never be pleased to see extreme behaviour, we know that our feelings can normally be coped with by

- sharing them with others
- reminding ourselves that we have our own sense of direction and do not simply respond emotionally to others' behaviour, and
- giving ourselves one or two timely pieces of advice - acting as 'my own best friend' when needed.

Rating: ………..

We are reticent to use punishment in our service. However, when necessary, mainly in connection with intrinsically reinforcing behaviour, we do use it, but remember that it is the behaviour that we are trying to punish (make less frequent) rather than the patient. This usually leads us to think of some ingenious "punishments" which hardly seem like punishment at all - more often it just seems like the natural consequence of the behaviour in question. In any event we always remember the RIP acronym.

Rating: ………..

We always ensure that we *monitor* the degree of specific extreme behaviour from individual clients, so that we can see the progress being made, and so can the client.

Rating: ………..

Chapter 33:

Self-Assessment Checklist:
Are You Really A RAIDer?

You might like to check out how you match up. Below is a series of statements which we call 'dream statements'. They describe perfection. Underneath each there is a space for you to give yourself a rating out of 100, the more the better.

I have a clear philosophy of care, known as RAIDing. It means I see the best in people ... I notice predominantly the *good* behaviour that clients emit, and acknowledge or recognise it just right. As this implies, I ignore, or at least play down, the difficult or disruptive behaviour.

Rating: ....

I know that the essence of RAIDing is to push green behaviour into the person. So if I see that someone reacts in a way that is bad for them when they are for example being wound up or being frustrated by something, I do my best to teach them a better way of responding.

Rating: ....

I also RAID in the sense of pushing as much reinforcement into the person's life as I can do. I know that the more reinforcing the person's life is, the less the extreme behaviour will ensue.

Rating: ....

I always recollect why the RAID approach works (building the client, maintaining a good relationship, providing a good model, and providing an appropriate means for our clients to obtain positive attention). This means I can apply it even in new situations.

Rating: ………..

I display the 'Appropriate' personality characteristics. Especially, I am empathic, constantly positive, energetic, patient, determined, and a team player. And I monitor my maintenance of these qualities!

Rating: ………..

I am intent on providing each person with the right level of relationship from which they can benefit, and I understand that without this relationship I am hardly 'in the game'.

Rating: ………..

I am excellent at ensuring that clients know exactly what is expected of them. I make sure they have a vivid picture of what they are meant to do, right from waking in the morning until going to bed at night, how they are meant to spend their time, what they are to do if they have problems or worries, and how they can best pursue treatment goals. This way, my clients feel secure and that they have a mastery over their time and their life. What is more, my colleagues and I have now all agreed on what is expected, so we are all pulling in the same direction.

Rating: ………..

In groups of two or more, I spot particularly those who are behaving *right,* and gently ensure that they are acknowledged. I am aware of the danger of winding up anyone who is behaving badly by doing this, but I do it subtly enough to avoid that danger!

Rating: ………..

I am terrific at giving feedback in a straightforward, constructive, friendly way. I realise that the point is for the person to know mainly when they are doing *right,* so they can do it again! I am also careful not to overdo it; I know people can have too much feedback, even if it's positive!

Rating: ………..

I am excellent in using positive words to describe aspects of clients' personality, to build their self-image and self-esteem.

Rating: ………..

I never tell people what not to do! Rather, I suggest - as gently and as tactfully as I can - what they *should* do, and if I can't think what they should do, I just keep quiet!

Rating: ………..

I avoid asking the obvious *'what shall we do when he comes out of his room in the middle of the night and smashes the place up?'* question, and instead ask a question of the *'how can we get him to sleep through the night?'"*type.

Rating: ………..

I am excellent at instilling a sense of the *future* in clients so they have a clear direction and know they are working towards what they want. I am also strong at encouraging and supporting them in achieving those goals.

Rating: ………..

When it is necessary I am well able to use the RAID 4-box functional analysis of extreme behaviour. I complete the forms objectively and thoroughly, analyse them later to properly determine what underlies the behaviour. I can then go on to choose a suitable intervention

Rating: ………..

When I can see the extreme behaviour serves a clear function for the person, I am ingenious at devising a more beneficial way that he or she can achieve that function. This is so even when the function is to obtain attention! I understand that all of us need attention, and it's just a matter of how we go about getting it! And anyway, I know that extreme behaviour can serve all sorts of functions; I am shrewd at working out what they might be, and helping the people achieve them in ways that are better for them.

Rating: ………..

I am good at working out what triggers the extreme behaviour, if anything (and I know there often is). When I have worked it out I know to
- get rid of the trigger, or
- teach the client how to cope with it, or
- reinforce the client when the trigger occurs and s/he doesn't respond badly.

Rating: ………..

I am first rate at judging if an issue really must be addressed. If so I choose a time when the client and I are likely to discuss things rationally with each other, I keep the conversation focused on future solutions rather than past problems, I ensure that we reach some kind of agreement, and I arrange to review progress later on.

Rating: ………..

I know how to handle my feelings when extreme behaviour does occur. Although I know that I will probably never be pleased to see extreme behaviour, I know that my feelings can normally be coped with by
- sharing them with others
- reminding myself that I have my own sense of direction and do not simply respond emotionally to others' behaviour, and

- giving myself one or two timely pieces of advice - acting as 'my own best friend' when needed.

Rating: ………..

I am reluctant to use punishment. However, when necessary, mainly in connection with intrinsically reinforcing behaviour, I do use it, but remember that it is the behaviour that I am trying to punish (make less frequent) rather than the patient. This usually leads me to think of some ingenious 'punishments' which hardly seem like punishment at all - more often it just seems like the natural consequence of the behaviour in question. In any event I always remember the RIP acronym.

Rating: ………..

I always ensure that we *monitor* the degree of specific extreme behaviour from individual clients, so that we can see the progress being made, and so can the client.

Rating: ………..

Well, whatever you scored, you can probably work on it! It is a good idea to rate yourself every week on the same day, say Friday afternoon. There are a lot of areas to focus on, and this keeps reminding us of them.